Bariatric Friendly Recipes

Gastric Bypass Cookbook, Gastric Sleeve Cookbook, Weight Loss Surgery Cookbook, Bariatric Cookbook

Richard P. Russel

Bariatric Friendly Recipes: Gastric Bypass Cookbook, Gastric Sleeve Cookbook, Weight Loss Surgery Cookbook, Bariatric Cookbook

Table of Contents

Book 1 - Gastric Bypass Cookbook

Quick And Easy Meals After Weight Loss Surgery (Gastric Sleeve, Obesity Related Diseases, Long Term Plan)

1 - Introduction

Gastric Sleeve Surgery

Gastric sleeve surgery is a non-reversible surgical operation designed to decrease the size of your stomach and help you lose weight. It is an important step you can take to achieve successful weight loss, especially if you are obese or severely overweight and have not lost that weight successfully even after following a diet plan, working out, or taking medicine.

Smaller is Better

Having a smaller stomach means you will be satisfied with what you are eating more quickly. Now that you have a smaller tummy, it also means you have to change certain things related to the way you eat, such as consuming foods in portion sizes that are smaller than what you have been used to so that you can easily reach your weight loss goals.

Making the Cut

In carrying out the gastric sleeve operation, the surgeon either goes for an open operation where he makes a big incision in your abdomen or uses the laparoscopic approach in which he makes a number of small incisions with the aid of a camera and small instruments.

Either way, you will end up having a large part of your stomach (more than half) removed, and with a banana-sized tube (thin vertical sleeve) left. To help your newly reduced stomach after the operation, surgical staples are put in place.

An Instant Fix It Is Not

Your doctor will generally consider you as a candidate for gastric sleeve surgery when your BMI (body mass index) hits the 40 or 40-plus mark. This operation is also an option your doctor might resort to if you suffer from a disabling or life-threatening condition on top of having a BMI of 35 or higher.

All of these sound hopeful, but you need to realize that gastric sleeve surgery is a weight loss tool, not an operation that will instantly fix your excess weight woes. Even with the help of going through a gastric sleeve surgical operation, you will still have to follow a healthy diet plan and engage in regular physical activity. Otherwise, you will just gain back all of that lost weight.

Pretty Effective

As shown in research studies, gastric sleeve surgery can help you people shed off more than ½ of their excess pounds.

Individuals who are more realistic in their weight loss goals and expectations also have a higher success in terms of the amount of weight lost, especially if they make sure to keep on eating their recommended diet plan, being physically active, and keeping their appointments with their health care/medical team.

The Ever After

What to eat will most likely be your greatest concern after going through your gastric sleeve surgery. Expect your doctor to provide you a detailed list of what you can and what you cannot eat after the operation. For the first post-surgery month, during which your body is on healing mode, you smaller stomach will only be able to hold soft foods as well as liquids in small amounts.

You need to keep hydrating your body during this period,

which you easily accomplish by sipping water all through the day. You will probably realize that your bowel movements become irregular after the operation – although this is a common outcome of gastric sleeve surgery, it is important that you avoid bowel movement straining and constipation.

You will find that you can gradually include solid foods into your after-surgery diet plan. Take extra care to really chew your food, and always stop eating anything the moment you feel full. This does take some getting used to, especially when you feel satisfied after consuming food in fewer quantities than what you have been accustomed to.

If you forget to chew your food well and keep on eating after you feel full, you may experience nausea and discomfort, which can sometimes be accompanied by vomiting. If you consume plenty of fruit juices, sodas, or other high-calorie beverages, you may be able to reach your weight loss goals.

And if you keep on overeating, your reduced stomach may get stretched, which will cancel out the benefits brought on by your gastric sleeve operation.

1 - INTRODUCTION

Your doctor may encourage you to seek the advice of a dietitian who can help you create and follow a healthy diet plan
that allows your body to lose weight while still getting adequate protein as well as vitamins and minerals. It is important to stick to your new diet and make sure to keep on
taking your recommended supplemental vitamins and minerals.

2 - Obesity-Related Diseases

Gastric sleeve surgery will not only help you lose weight, it will also help you avoid suffering from various health conditions related to obesity, such as type 2 diabetes, gallbladder disease, gout, stroke and heart disease, cancer, osteoarthritis, and sleep apnea. A person is considered obese when he or she weighs at least twenty percent more than his or her normal weight.

Diabetes (type 2)

Most individuals suffering from diabetes (type 2) are usually also suffering from overweight or obesity. Reduce your risk of developing this condition by shedding off those excess pounds, following a balanced diet plan, engaging in regular physical exercise, and making sure to get enough sleep.

If you do suffer from diabetes (type 2), make sure to lose weight as well as get more physical exercise so that you can get your blood sugar levels stabilized. When your body is more active, you will find that you have less need for taking your medication to treat diabetes.

Gallbladder disease

Being overweight increases your chances of developing gallstones and gallbladder disease. Keep in mind though, that losing weight may actually cause your body to form gallstones. To get around this irony, make sure to lose weight following a target rate of no more than one pound per week.

Gout

Your joints are the ones affected by gout, and this disease is a result of your blood having high levels of uric acid. All that excess uric acid in your bloodstream can crystallize and get lodged in your joints.

In the same ironic vein as the gallstones, your gout condition may actually flare up when you experience sudden weight loss. To get around this problem, make sure to get your doctor's advice on how to lose weight.

Stroke and heart disease

Carrying excess weight in your body can increase your risk of having high cholesterol levels and suffering from high blood pressure, both of which can also may it more likely for you to have a stroke or get heart disease.

Fortunately, you can lose weight to decrease your risk of suffering from stroke or heart disease. Even if you just lose five to ten percent of your weight, it is enough so that your risk of developing heart disease will be decreased.

Cancer

Aside from being linked by a number of studies to pancreatic cancer, ovarian cancer, and cancer of the gallbladder, obesity is also linked to colon cancer as well as cancers of the kidney, esophagus, breast (post-menopause), and endometrium or uterine lining.

Osteoarthritis

When you have osteoarthritis, your back, hip, or knee is affected. Osteoarthritis results from your excess weight placing added pressure on the said joints, which cause their cartilage (joint-cushioning tissue) to get worn away. By losing extra weight, you help ease the stress on your joints in the lower back, hips, and knees, as well as improve your osteoarthritis symptoms.

Sleep apnea

Being overweight can lead to a breathing condition called sleep apnea, in which the individual affected snores heavily in his or her sleep and then suddenly stops breathing for a brief moment. This can cause you to feel sleepy during the day as well as increase your risk of having stroke and heart disease. If you have sleep apnea, losing weight can help you improve your condition.

3 - Long-Term Habits

Undergoing a gastric bypass surgery helps you control your calorie intake, adopt proper eating habits, and achieve your weight loss goals. The following tips should enable you to eat and thrive after surviving your surgery.

Take enough liquids (six to eight cups daily is recommended) to hydrate your body properly. Try the following:

- Drink 1 cup of fluid over an hour.

- Don't drink anything within thirty minutes to one hour of a meal.

- Make sure to slowly sip your allowed liquids.

- Never use a straw when drinking your liquids.

Consume adequate amounts of protein.

Supplement your gastric bypass diet with the necessary vitamins and minerals once your doctor allows you to. Make sure to take calcium, iron, zinc, and B12 supplements.

Steer clear of all forms of high-calorie foods and drinks.

Eat your food really slowly and thoroughly.

Once you feel full, stop eating. You will know you are full when:

- You feel pressure in the middle just beneath the rib cage.

- You feel nauseous.

- You feel a shoulder or upper chest pain.

Begin each meal with protein. Your pouch will eventually expand, and then you will only need to consume three meals plus one to two protein-rich snacks every day.

Avoid the following foods, which you may find difficult to handle, after the surgery:

- Peas, dried beans, cabbage, celery, corn, and other fibrous vegetables; raw vegetables; and mushrooms

- Coconut, dried fruits, grapefruit and orange membranes, and all fruit peels/skins

- Pork chops and other fatty meat cuts, as well as fried

meats, fish, and poultry

- Hamburger, steak, and other meat substitutes

- Starches including granola, non-toasted bread (white/whole grain), cereals (whole grain), bran and bran cereals, popcorn, and noodle/vegetable soups

- Sweets like desserts, sweetened fruit juice, sweetened beverages, jam/jelly, and candy

- Nuts and seeds

- Pickles

- Spiced foods and other highly seasoned foods

- Carbonated drinks

Depending on your tolerance and making sure to advance gradually, follow the 5-Phase Weight Loss Surgery Diet in the next chapter.

4 - 5-Phase Weight Loss Surgery Diet

1st Phase – Clear Liquid Diet

1. Until your surgeon approves it, you should not consume any food or drink any beverage after your gastric sleeve operation.

2. As soon as your surgeon does approve, expect to drink water, broth (clear), apple juice (unsweetened), tea (decaffeinated), and other non-red fluids. You can drink only one ounce or thirty milliliters of liquid per hour. If you find that you can handle drinking one ounce per hour, you can then drink up to two ounces or sixty milliliters of liquid per hour the next day.

3. Never use a straw, which will cause you to drink your liquids too quickly. "Slowly" should be your keyword when it comes to drinking liquids.

4. Know that you are not expected to drink every liquid brought to you down to the last drop. As soon as your stomach feels full, stop drinking.

5. You may experience nausea, vomiting, or both during your first post-gastric sleeve surgery days. This is not uncommon and is no cause for alarm – just remember to drink slowly. Immediately contact a nurse if the vomiting or nauseous feeling does not go away.

2nd Phase – Full Liquid Diet

1. The day you are discharged from the hospital is the day you can get started on your full liquid diet phase.

2. Unless your surgeon, as well as a dietitian, advises otherwise, you need to be in the 2nd phase (full liquid) diet for a period of one to two weeks.

3. Keep nausea and vomiting at bay by making sure to slowly drink your liquids. See to it that you sip two ounces or one-fourth cup of liquid in more than thirty minutes. But you should force yourself to drink up everything – stop as soon as you feel full.

4. Between your high-protein drinks, make sure to take in a minimum of six to eight cups of drinking water or beverages that are low in calories. Steer clear of citrus, caffeinated, and carbonated drinks.

5. As instructed, do not forget to take your supplemental calcium, multivitamins, and minerals.

6. Monitor your intake of all high-protein drinks, including their kinds and amounts. Make sure to reach your target of sixty grams of protein per day.

3rd Phase – Puree Diet

1. Once you are done with your one- to two-weeks' worth of full liquid diet, you can gradually include thicker consistency-foods to your gastric sleeve diet. Make sure to blend or puree all your foods for the following two weeks to the consistency of baby foods.

2. You have the option of incorporating your full liquid diet foods into your puree (3rd phase) diet.

3. Remember to always chew your foods carefully, which will help in preventing feelings of nausea or blockage. Check first if you can handle eating one to two tablespoons of pureed foods at a time. See to it that your every meal is composed of just two to four tablespoons or one-eighth to one-fourth cup of food.

4. Never forget to consume protein first in each of your meals. Make sure to get at least sixty grams of protein into your body on a daily basis.

5. Hydrate your body by making sure to drink six to eight cups of water as well as low-calorie drinks before and after meals. You can have a portion of your overall fluid intake consist of one-percent or fat-free milk.

6. Keep monitoring your protein intake on a daily basis, taking note of of their kinds and amounts.

4th Phase – Soft Diet

1. After having done the two-week long puree diet, there is no longer a need for you to keep blending your food. Slowly introduce soft-consistency foods to your diet, making sure you can easily cut them with a fork.

2. Keep in mind that the soft (4th phase) diet lasts for two weeks, during which you can try eating new food one at a time.

3. You will find controlling your portions much easier if

you eat off smaller plates. It also helps to use baby spoons and bay forks. Don't forget to stop eating as soon as you feel full.

4. Make sure your body is always hydrated. Between meals, strive to drink six to eight cups of water/low-calorie drinks. But do not drink your liquids with your meals – you can have your liquids half an hour before and half an hour after your meal.

5. Remember to keep taking your prescribed supplements.

6. Keep monitoring your kinds and amounts of protein consumed each day. You should aim to eat at least sixty grams of protein every day.

5th Phase – Regular Diet

1. You should be ready to follow the regular (5th phase) diet after two weeks on your soft (4th phase) diet. You may be able to take up the regular diet one month or two months after surgery, depending on your post-gastric sleeve surgery body's progress.

2. You can keep on slowly introducing new foods during this phase of your diet. You may add vegetables and fruits, but you might be better off avoiding any fruit skins and membranes.

3. Make sure to keep your diet low in fats and free of simple sugars. Remember that your protein consumption should be sixty grams or more daily. To help you lose weight successfully, keep your intake of calories in the range of eight hundred to one thousand two hundred per day (consult your dietitian on the appropriate amount of calories that suits your needs).

4. Remember to keep eating five to six small meals daily. It may be better for you to have three small meals as well as one to two snacks (high-protein) per day as your new stomach expands.

5. Keep taking your prescribed supplements (you will be taking them for life).

6. Always hydrate yourself by drinking six to eight cups of water as well as low-calorie drinks every day.

7. Keep monitoring your daily food consumption as well as activities, taking note of your calorie intake, protein intake, fluid intake, supplements, and physical activity.

8. Keep track of any warning signs your body may be sending. Your new stomach may not be comfortable taking in some food or have yet to get used to portion sizes right. Make sure to watch out for these symptoms and consequently modify your diet:

Feeling full

Prior to your gastric sleeve surgery, it felt normal for you to feel full after eating. Post-surgery, however, you should strive to avoid feeling full before you stop eating. This is an effective way for you to steer clear of any vomiting problems.

Nausea/vomiting

A food you ate may be the reason for your nausea or vomiting, although being dehydrated can also play a part, especially when it occurs quickly and rarely. Make sure to note the food you ate in your food journal for future reference, and always drink sixty-four ounces of fluids on a daily basis.

Bloating/cramping

Certain food may be the culprit for your bloating or cramping. Take note of what you ate and exclude it from your diet; otherwise, cook it using another cooking method.

Chest pain/discomfort

Write down the food you ate as well as its amount in your food journal right away. If your chest pain or discomfort does not subside immediately or if it keeps coming back after every meal, call your doctor as soon as possible.

Abdominal pain/continual vomiting

This warrants an immediate call to your doctor. This could be a signal of surgery complications, so get medical attention right away. It may be nothing, or it may be serious, but it is always better to be safe than sorry when it comes to your health.

5 - Chicken Recipes

Balsamic Rosemary Chicken Roast

Ingredients:

- Rosemary, fresh (1 tablespoon) OR dry (1 teaspoon)

- Rosemary sprigs, fresh (8 pieces)

- Olive oil, extra virgin (1 tablespoon)

- Brown sugar (1 teaspoon)

- Chicken, whole (4 pounds)

- Garlic clove (1 piece)

- Black pepper, freshly ground (1/8 teaspoon)

- Balsamic vinegar (1/2 cup)

Directions:

1. Set the oven at 350 degrees to preheat.

2. Place the garlic and rosemary (both minced) in a medium bowl. Mix well and set aside.

3. Loosely separate the skin of the chicken from its flesh. Rub the flesh with the olive oil before rubbing with the rosemary-garlic mixture as well. Sprinkle on the black pepper and then fill the chicken's cavity with two sprigs of rosemary.

4. Truss the chicken before placing inside a roasting pan. Roast in the preheated oven for about one hour and twenty minutes, making sure to baste the chicken frequently with the juices in the pan. Once the juices run clear and the meat is browned, remove the chicken from the oven and place on a platter. Set aside.

5. Meanwhile, pour the balsamic vinegar as well as brown sugar into a saucepan. Heat on medium and stir the mixture without boiling or until the sugar is completely dissolved.

6. Remove the skin off the chicken after carving it. Pour the vinegar mixture onto the carved chicken pieces, then top with the rest of the rosemary sprigs.

7. Serve right away.

Braised Mushrooms and Chicken

Ingredients:

- Black pepper, freshly ground (1/2 teaspoon)

- Chicken legs, skinless (2 pieces)

- Stock/broth, chicken/vegetable, low sodium (3/4 cup)

- Thyme, fresh, chopped (2 tablespoons)

- Thyme sprigs, fresh (3 pieces)

- Chicken breast halves, bone-in, sliced crosswise (4 pieces)

- Mushrooms, white button, small, brushed clean (1 pound)

- Balsamic vinegar (2 tablespoons)

- Flour, all-purpose (1/4 cup)

- Olive oil, extra virgin (1 ½ tablespoons)

- Chicken thighs, bone-in, skinless (2 pieces)

- Shallots, chopped (1 tablespoon)

- Pearl onions, peeled (1/2 pound)

- Red wine, dry (1/2 cup)

- Salt (1/4 teaspoon)

Directions:

1. Place the flour in a small bowl. Add the pepper (1/4 teaspoon) and mix well.

2. Add the chicken pieces to the seasoned flour, turning to coat them evenly on all sides.

3. Heat a large saucepan (heavy bottomed) on medium-high before adding the oil. Add the coated chicken pieces and cook for two to three minutes on each side or until cooked through and browned. Place on a platter and set aside.

4. Stir shallot into the same saucepan. Cook for one minute or until softened, then stir in the mushrooms.

Cook for an additional three to four minutes or until lightly browned.

5. Add the onions, stir well, and cook for another two to three minutes or until a bit browned.

6. Pour in the wine and stock. Stir and scrape until the pan is deglazed. Add back the chicken pieces and allow to boil before covering and turning the heat down to low. Simmer the mixture for about forty to forty-five minutes or until the veggies and chicken are tenderly cooked.

7. Add in the chopped thyme, salt (1 teaspoon), remaining pepper (1/4 teaspoon), and vinegar. Stir to combine.

8. Arrange the vegetables in warmed individual bowls. Add the chicken pieces (2 pieces per bowl) on top before garnishing with sprigs of thyme.

9. Serve and enjoy.

Cheesy Chicken Wrap

Ingredients:

- Onions, chopped (1/4 cup)

- Tortilla, whole wheat, low carb (1 piece)

- Mushrooms, sliced (1/4 cup)

- Hot chili peppers, pickled, sliced (2 teaspoons)

- Chicken breast, skinless, boneless, w/ fat trimmed out (1/4 pound)

- Green pepper, sliced (1/4 cup)

- Swiss cheese, wedged slice, ¾-ounce (1 piece)

Directions:

1. Pound the chicken breast until about a quarter-inch thick, then slice thinly into strips. Set aside.

2. Heat a large skillet (nonstick) on medium before misting lightly with cooking spray. Once hot, add the

onion as well as the chicken strips. Cook for about five minutes or until the chicken pieces are cooked through and the onions are fragrant and translucent.

3. Stir in the mushrooms and green peppers. Cook for two minutes or until softened, then set aside.

4. Insert the tortilla between two paper towels (dampened with a little water). Heat in the microwave for about twenty seconds, then lay flat on a plate.

5. Spread cheese evenly down the center of the warm tortilla, then top with the chicken strips as well as the mushrooms, onions, peppers, and chili peppers.

6. Fold the tortilla before serving. Enjoy.

Chicken and Cabbage Salad

Ingredients:

- Chicken breasts, boneless, skinless (1 ¼ pounds)

- Lemongrass stalks, w/ 6-inches bottom only, sliced thinly (2 pieces)

- Soy sauce, reduced sodium (1 tablespoon)

- Olive oil, extra virgin (3 tablespoons)

- Peanuts, dry roasted, unsalted, crushed (1 table-spoon)

- Spring onion, sliced into lengthwise halves (1 piece)

- Green onions, sliced thinly (2 pieces)

- Rice vinegar (2 tablespoons)

- Peanut butter (1 tablespoon)

- Cabbage head, green, small (1/2 piece)

- Stock/broth, chicken/vegetable, reduced sodium (2 cups)

- Ginger, fresh, sliced thinly, ½-inch (1 piece)

- Cilantro sprigs, fresh (3 pieces)

- Cilantro, fresh, chopped (3 tablespoons)

- Lime juice, freshly squeezed (2 tablespoons)

- Fish sauce (1 tablespoon)

- Shallot, minced (1 tablespoon)

- Garlic clove (1 piece)

- Spinach (1/2 bunch)

- Carrot, large, peeled, sliced into lengthwise halves, cut diagonally into thin slices (1 piece)

Directions:

1. Fill a large saucepan with the stock as well as ginger, cilantro, lemongrass, and green onion. Stir to combine and heat on high. Allow the mixture to boil before reducing heat to low, then simmer for about five minutes.

2. Stir in the chicken breasts. Return the heat to high to allow the mixture to boil again.

3. Turn heat back to low and let the mixture simmer for about three minutes. Remove from heat, uncover, and let the chicken sit in the stock until slightly cooled.

4. Pour the stock into a large bowl and set aside. Meanwhile, shred the chicken into half-inch-thick and two-inch-long strips. Place in the refrigerator.

5. After straining off the solids from the cooled stock, pour the stock (1½ cups) back into the saucepan. Heat on medium-high and allow the stock to boil for five to six minutes, uncovered, or until reduced to 1/3 its original volume.

6. Fill a blender with the reduced stock. Add in the vinegar, soy sauce, lime juice, fish sauce, garlic, shallot, and peanut butter. Process until well-combined and evenly smooth. Gradually stream in the olive oil as you keep the blender motor running. Set aside the now-thinner dressing.

7. Meanwhile, discard the spinach stems and core the cabbage. Chop the spinach crosswise into quarter-inch strips and place in a large bowl; repeat with the cabbage (add to the same bowl as the spinach).

8. Add the shredded chicken to the spinach-cabbage bowl. Add in the carrot, green onions, and cilantro as

well. Gently toss to combine.

9. Top the salad with the prepared dressing (1/2 portion) before dividing among salad plates.

10. Serve garnished with peanuts, alongside the remaining dressing.

Easy Chicken Rollantini

Ingredients:

- Breadcrumbs, whole wheat, Italian seasoned (1/2 cup)

- Ricotta cheese, part skim (6 tablespoons)

- Egg whites, divided (6 tablespoons)

- Marinara sauce (1 cup)

- Chicken breast cutlets, 3-ounces, pounded until thin (8 pieces)

- Parmesan cheese, grated, divided (1/4 cup)

- Spinach, frozen, thawed, squeezed of liquid until dry

(5 ounces)

- Mozzarella cheese, part skim, shredded, divided (6 ounces)

- Cooking spray, nonstick

Directions:

1. Set the oven at 450 degrees to preheat.

2. Meanwhile, use cooking spray to grease a glass baking dish (9x13). Set aside.

3. Place chicken cutlets in a large bowl. Add the pepper and salt; rub on the chicken pieces to season well. Set aside.

4. Place the breadcrumbs and Parmesan cheese (2 tablespoons) in a medium bowl. Stir to combine before setting aside.

5. Fill another medium bowl with the egg whites (1/4 cup). Set aside.

6. Place mozzarella cheese (1 ½ ounces) in a large bowl.

Add the remaining Parmesan cheese as well as ricotta cheese and remaining egg whites (2 tablespoons).

7. Arrange the seasoned cutlets on a large tray. Add the spinach-cheese mixture (2 tablespoons) on top of each chicken piece, making sure to spread evenly.

8. Roll each chicken cutlet as you loosely keep their seams down, then use a toothpick to secure each cutlet.

9. Place each rolled chicken piece in the egg white mixture, then dredge in the breadcrumbs mixture. Arrange all coated chicken rolls in the prepped baking dish and then lightly coat with cooking spray (non-stick).

10. Place in the oven to bake for twenty-five minutes. Once done, remove from the oven and smother with the marinara sauce. Top with the shredded mozzarella cheese and return to the oven to bake for another three minutes.

11. Once the cheese on top has melted, remove the dish from the oven and sprinkle with Parmesan cheese.

Serve immediately.

Healthy Chicken Pizza

Ingredients:

- Pizza crust, thin, 12-inch (1 piece)

- Chicken breast, cooked, sliced into one-inch thickness, w/ visible fat trimmed off (4 ounces)

- Tomato, sliced (1 piece)

- Mozzarella cheese, reduced fat, shredded (1 cup)

- Tomato sauce, w/out added salt (1 cup)

- Green pepper rings (8 pieces)

- Mushrooms, sliced (1 cup)

- Barbecue sauce, homemade (4 tablespoons)

Directions:

1. Set the oven to 400 degrees to preheat.

2. Cover the entire surface of the pizza crust with the sauce, making sure to evenly spread the sauce. After drizzling the barbecue sauce on top, sprinkle with the shredded mozzarella cheese.

3. Place in the oven to bake for about twelve to fourteen minutes.

4. Once done, remove from the oven and slice into eight portions.

5. Serve and enjoy.

Smokin' Chicken Fajitas

Ingredients:

- Garlic cloves, minced (2 pieces)

- Onion, large, sliced (1 piece)

- Salsa (1/2 cup)

- Cumin, ground (1/2 teaspoon)

- Bell pepper, sweet, red, slivered (1/2 piece)

- Cheese, low fat, shredded (1/2 cup)

- Lime juice, freshly squeezed (1/4 cup)

- Chili powder (1 teaspoon)

- Chicken breasts, skinless, boneless, sliced into quarter-inch strips (3 pounds)

- Bell pepper, green sweet, slivered (1/2 piece)

- Tortillas, whole wheat, 8" (12 pieces)

- Sour cream, fat free (1/2 cup)

Directions:

1. Place chicken strips in a large mixing bowl. Add the slivered bell peppers, minced garlic, ground cumin, chili powder, and lime juice. Toss until well-combined and the chicken strips are evenly coated.

2. Cover the bowl and place in the refrigerator. Allow the chicken to marinate for about fifteen minutes.

3. Heat a large saucepan on medium after spraying gen-

erously with nonstick cooking spray. Add the marinated chicken and cook for about three minutes or until cooked through.

4. Add the peppers and onions. Stir and cook for three to five minutes or until soft and fragrant.

5. Spoon equal portions of the prepared chicken mixture onto each tortilla.

6. Top each fajita with two teaspoons each of salsa, sour cream, and shredded cheese before rolling up.

7. Serve and enjoy.

Spinach Stuffed Cajun Chicken

Ingredients:

- Jack cheese, reduced fat, shredded (3 ounces)

- Cajun seasoning (2 tablespoons) – see below

- Chicken breasts, skinless, boneless (1 pound)

- Spinach, frozen, thawed, drained OR fresh cooked (1

cup)

- Bread crumbs, whole wheat (1 tablespoon)

Cajun seasoning:

- Oregano (1/4 teaspoon)

- Onion powder (3/4 teaspoon)

- White pepper (1/4 teaspoon)

- Black pepper (1/4 teaspoon)

- Thyme (1/4 teaspoon)

- Paprika (3/4 tablespoon)

- Garlic powder (3/4 teaspoon)

- Cayenne pepper (1/2 teaspoon)

- Cumin (1/4 teaspoon)

Directions:

1. Set the oven at 350 degrees to preheat. Meanwhile,

use tin foil to line a baking sheet; set aside.

2. Pound the chicken on a cutting board until about a quarter of an inch in thickness.

3. Place the spinach in a large bowl. Add the Jack cheese, pepper, and salt, then toss to combine.

4. Place the breadcrumbs in a medium bowl. Add the Cajun seasoning and mix well.

5. Top each chicken breast with the spinach mixture (1/4 cup) before rolling tightly and securing the seams with toothpicks.

6. Brush olive oil onto each stuffed chicken roll, then sprinkle with the prepared breadcrumbs mixture. After making sure each chicken roll is evenly covered, add the rest of the cheese and spinach on top.

7. Arrange the stuffed chicken pieces inside the lined baking sheet and place in the oven to bake for about thirty-five to forty minutes or until the chicken pieces are completely cooked.

8. Remove the baking sheet from the oven, take out the toothpicks, and transfer the stuffed chicken onto a platter.

9. Slice into medallions and serve right away.

10. Enjoy.

Tasty Chicken Lettuce Wraps

Ingredients:

- Water chestnuts, drained, minced (8 ounces)

- Soy sauce, low sodium (2 teaspoons)

- Onion, minced (1 cup)

- Sesame oil, toasted (1 teaspoon)

- Hoisin sauce (2 tablespoons)

- Stevia (2 packets)

- Green onion, whole, chopped (1 piece)

- Bamboo shoots, drained, minced (8 ounces)

- Cooking wine, sherry (3 tablespoons)

- Peanut butter, unsalted (1 tablespoon)

- Hot pepper sauce (2 teaspoons)

- Garlic, minced (1 tablespoon)

- Chicken breast, ground (1/2 pound)

- Salt (1/4 teaspoon)

- Butter lettuce leaves, small (8 pieces)

- Cucumber, small, seeded, sliced into one-inch strips (1 piece)

Directions:

1. Place the bamboo shoots in a large bowl. Add the sherry, peanut butter, hot pepper sauce, hoisin sauce, soy sauce, sugar substitute, and water chestnuts. Stir to combine before setting aside.

2. Heat a large skillet (nonstick) on medium after misting it with cooking spray. Stir in the onion to cook for

about four minutes or until softened and fragrant.

3. Stir in the garlic; cook for one minute before turning the heat up to medium-high. Stir in the salt, ginger, and ground chicken. Cook for three to four minutes or until the chicken is cooked through and broken up.

4. Stir in the bamboo shoot mixture and cook for an additional two to three minutes. Add the toasted sesame oil. Give everything a good stir before turning off the heat.

5. Top each lettuce leaf with equal portions of the chicken mixture, then top with cucumber and chopped green onion.

6. Serve right away.

Yummy Chicken Casserole

Ingredients:

- Chicken breast, skinless, cooked, cubed (1 cup)

- Mushrooms, canned (4 ounces)

- Soup, cream of chicken, 98-percent fat free (10 ½ ounces)

- Pepper, freshly cracked (1/4 teaspoon)

- Garlic powder (1/4 teaspoon)

- Onion powder (1/4 teaspoon)

- Pasta, whole wheat, uncooked (1/2 cup) OR cooked (1 cup)

- Mixed vegetables, frozen (2 cups)

- Cheddar cheese, 2-percent milk, reduced fat, shredded (1 cup)

- Water (3/4 cup)

Directions:

1. Set the oven at 350 degrees to preheat.

2. Use cooking spray to coat a casserole dish (9x13).

3. Follow package directions in cooking the vegetables and pasta.

4. Place the chicken in a large mixing bowl. Add the mushrooms, cheese (1/2 cup), water, soup, and milk as well as the cooked vegetables and pasta. Gently toss to combine, making sure the veggies and pasta are evenly coated.

5. Stir in the onion powder, garlic powder, and pepper before pouring the entire mixture into the prepped casserole dish. Top with the remaining cheese and place in the preheated oven.

6. Bake for about twenty-five to thirty minutes or until the cheese turns bubbly and golden.

7. Serve and enjoy.

6 - Fish Recipes

Alfredo Salmon

Ingredients:

- Salmon fillets, 4-ounces (4 pieces)

- Garlic cloves, minced (4 pieces)

- Salt (1/2 teaspoon)

- Broth, chicken, low sodium, warmed (1 cup)

- Parmesan cheese, grated (1/2 cup)

- Olive oil, extra virgin (1 tablespoon)

- Milk, skim (2 cups)

- Flour, all purpose (3 tablespoons)

- Black pepper, freshly ground (1/4 teaspoon)

Directions:

1. Heat a medium-size saucepan (nonstick) on medium before adding the olive oil.

2. Stir in the garlic and cook for two minutes or until fragrant.

3. Add the flour, stirring continuously until it thickens into a paste.

4. Pour in the warmed chicken broth and whisk well to combine.

5. Stir in the milk along with the pepper and salt.

6. Reduce heat to low and allow the mixture to cook until nicely thickened and smooth.

7. Add the Parmesan cheese; stir into the mixture before serving immediately.

Barbecued Salmon Roast

Ingredients:

- Lemon juice, freshly squeezed (2 tablespoons)

- Lemon rind, grated (2 teaspoons)

- Cinnamon (1/4 teaspoon)

- Brown sugar (2 tablespoons)

- Salt (1/2 teaspoon)

- Pineapple juice (1/4 cup)

- Salmon fillets, 6-ounces (4 pieces)

- Chili powder (4 teaspoons)

- Cumin, ground (3/4 teaspoon)

Directions:

1. Set the oven at 400 degrees to preheat.

2. Fill a large Ziploc bag with the pineapple juice, brown sugar, and salmon fillets. Gently toss inside the bag to combine, then place in the refrigerator to marinate for one hour, turning the bag halfway.

3. Once the salmon fillets are done marinating, take out of the bag (discard the remaining marinade) and transfer onto a plate.

4. Stir the rest of the ingredients together in a large

bowl. Once combined, rub over the salmon fillets.

5. Arrange the fillets inside the prepped baking dish. Place in the oven to bake for about twelve to fifteen minutes or until done.

6. Garnish with sliced lemon and serve immediately.

Broiled Roughy Fillets

Ingredients:

- Lemon wedges, medium (8 pieces)

- Dijon mustard (1 tablespoon)

- Pepper, freshly ground (1/4 teaspoon)

- Lemon juice, freshly squeezed (3 tablespoons)

- Olive oil, extra virgin (1 tablespoon)

- Roughy fillets, orange, 4-ounces (4 pieces)

Directions:

1. Tent a broiler pan's rack with tin foil before spraying

with nonstick cooking spray. Set aside.

2. Pour olive oil into a medium bowl. Add the mustard, ground pepper, and lemon juice. Stir to combine.

3. Arrange the roughy fillets on the prepped rack. Take ½ of the mustard mixture (set aside the rest for using later) and brush on the fillets.

4. Cook the fillets under the broiler for about five minutes or until the flesh easily flakes.

5. Sprinkle the remaining mustard mixture on the broiled roughy fillets; season with pepper and salt.

6. Garnish with lemon wedges before serving immediately.

7. Enjoy.

Cornmeal Crusted Fish Fillets

Ingredients:

- Olive oil, extra virgin (2 teaspoons)

- Cornmeal, yellow (3 tablespoons)

- Celery seeds, ground (1/4 teaspoon)

- Salt (1 pinch)

- Fish fillets (8 ounces)

- Parsley, chopped (1 ½ tablespoons)

- Black pepper, freshly ground (1/4 teaspoon)

Directions:

1. After cleaning and rinsing the fish fillets, and checking if no bones are left in their flesh, gently pat dry with paper towels. Set aside on a plate.

2. Place the cornmeal in a large bowl. Add the chopped parsley, pepper, celery seed, and salt. Stir to combine.

3. Pour the cornmeal mixture on top of the fish fillets. Make sure all sides of the fish are covered before carefully pressing the cornmeal onto the fillets.

4. Meanwhile, heat a nonstick skillet on medium before

adding the olive oil. Once heated through, add the fillets and cook for about two to three minutes on each side or until crisp and brown on the outside and flaky on the inside.

5. Serve and enjoy.

Dill Relished Bass

Ingredients:

- Sea bass fillets, white, 4-ounces (4 pieces)

- Baby capers, pickled, drained (1 teaspoon)

- Dijon mustard (1 teaspoon)

- White onion, chopped (1 ½ tablespoons)

- Dill, fresh, chopped (1 ½ teaspoons)

- Lemon juice, freshly squeezed (1 teaspoon)

- Lemon, sliced into quarters (1 piece)

Directions:

1. Set the oven to 375 degrees to preheat.

2. Meanwhile, fill a medium bowl with the dill, mustard, capers, lemon juice, and onion. Stir to combine.

3. Cut 4 squares of aluminum foil. Fill each square with one sea bass fillet and moisten with some lemon juice. Top with the dill mixture (1/4 portion per fillet) before wrapping the ends of the foil around the fillet.

4. Bake in the oven for about ten to twelve minutes or until opaque and cooked through.

5. Serve and enjoy.

Easy and Crunchy Tuna Patties

Ingredients:

- Egg whites (4 pieces)

- Onion, minced (1 tablespoon)

- Carrot, grated (1/4 cup)

- Pepper, freshly cracked (1/4 teaspoon)

- Dill (1/4 teaspoon)

- Mustard, dried (1/4 teaspoon)

- Tuna, canned, packed in water (12 ounces)

- Water chestnuts/ red pepper/ capers, chopped (1/4 cup)

- Crackers, wheat, thin, crushed (16 pieces)

Directions:

1. Place the tuna and all the remaining ingredients in a large bowl. Toss to combine.

2. Mold the tuna mixture into 8 equal sized patties.

3. Use cooking spray (nonstick) to coat a skillet (medium size). Heat on medium before adding the tuna patties.

4. Cook for about two to three minutes on each side or until cooked through and golden brown.

5. Serve and enjoy.

Greek Yogurt Salmon Fillets

Ingredients:

- Greek yogurt, plain, nonfat (1 cup)

- Garlic powder (1 teaspoon)

- Seasoning salt (1 ½ teaspoons)

- Salmon fillets, 4-ounces (4 pieces)

- Parmesan cheese, grated (1/2 cup)

- Pepper, freshly cracked (1/2 teaspoon)

Directions:

1. Set the oven to 375 degrees to preheat.

2. Place the cheese in a large bowl. Add the seasonings and Greek yogurt. Stir to combine.

3. Use foil to line a baking sheet, then lightly coat with cooking spray.

4. Dip the salmon fillets in the Greek yogurt mixture,

making sure they are evenly coated.

5. Arrange the coated fillets on the prepped baking sheet. Bake in the oven for forty-five minutes or until done.

6. Serve and enjoy.

Lemon-Caper Cod

Ingredients:

- Lemons (2 pieces)

- Tap water, hot (1 cup)

- Flour, all purpose (1 tablespoon)

- Cod fillets, 6-ounces (4 pieces)

- Bouillon granules, chicken flavored, low sodium (1 teaspoon)

- Butter, soft (1 tablespoon)

- Capers, rinsed, drained (4 teaspoons)

Directions:

1. Set the oven at 350 degrees to preheat.

2. Meanwhile, use cooking spray to lightly coat 4 foil squares on the surface. Set a single piece of cod fillet at the center of each foil square, then drizzle with lemon juice from half a piece of lemon. Slice the remaining half piece of lemon and place on top of the fish pieces.

3. Seal each of the filled foil square before placing in the oven. Bake for about twenty minutes or until the fish pieces are cooked through and opaque.

4. Meanwhile, carefully remove the peel off the other lemon, making sure none of the pith is removed as well. Cut the removed peel into quarter-inch-wide slices and place in a small bowl.

5. Pour hot tap water into another small bowl. Stir in the granulated chicken bouillon; once all the granules are completely dissolved, set aside.

6. Place the flour in a large bowl. Add the butter and stir

to combine. Once evenly mixed, pour into a saucepan (heavy bottomed). Heat on medium and stir the flour-butter mixture continuously. Once thickened, stir in the capers and immediately turn off the heat.

7. Pour the thickened flour-butter mixture on top of the fish. Add the lemon peel slices and serve right away.

Salmon with Mushroom Gravy

Ingredients:

- Sage, fresh, w/ stem discarded, chopped finely (2 tablespoons)

- Milk, skim (1 cup)

- Salmon fillets, 4-ounces (4 pieces)

- Soup, cream of mushroom, unsalted, divided (4 cups)

- Thyme, fresh, w/ stem discarded, chopped finely (2 tablespoons)

- Cornstarch (1/4 cup)

Directions:

1. Pour the cream of mushroom soup into a large saucepan. Heat on medium and stir continuously until heated through. Stir in the thyme and sage, then simmer until the soup is reduced to about ¾ its original volume. Turn off the heat and set aside.

2. Fill a medium bowl with the milk. Stir in the cornstarch. Once well-combined, pour into the simmering mushroom soup and stir well.

3. Allow the mixture to boil before stirring continuously for about three to five minutes or until thickened. Transfer into a gravy boat and set aside.

4. Meanwhile, heat a large saucepan (nonstick). Add a little olive oil and the salmon fillets. Cook for two to three minutes on each side or until cooked through and flaky.

5. Serve the salmon fillets smothered with the mushroom gravy.

Teriyaki Grouper

Ingredients:

- Garlic, minced (1/2 teaspoon)

- Teriyaki sauce, reduced sodium (1 tablespoon)

- Grouper fillets, 4-ounces (2 pieces)

- Italian seasoning (1/4 teaspoon)

- Lemon wedges (2 pieces)

Directions:

1. Fill a medium bowl with the garlic and teriyaki sauce. Whisk well to combine, then brush this mixture on all sides of the grouper fillets.

2. Use cooking spray to lightly coat a baking pan. Add the teriyaki-brushed grouper fillets at the bottom.

3. Cover the pan and place in the refrigerator to marinate for a minimum of fifteen minutes.

4. Meanwhile, turn on the broiler (grill) to preheat before positioning the rack about four inches away from the source of heat.

5. Cook the fish for about five to ten minutes or until the flesh is opaque and slightly firm.

6. Once done, take the fish out of the broiler and immediately sprinkle with the lemon juice from one wedge as well as Italian seasoning.

7. Serve and enjoy.

7 - Shrimp Recipes

Creamy Shrimp Salad

Ingredients:

- Pickle juice (1 tablespoon)

- Eggs, powdered (1 tablespoon)

- Mayonnaise, homemade (1 ½ tablespoons)

- Shrimp, large, shelled, deveined, poached (6 ounces)

Directions:

1. Set the poached shrimp on a platter. Set aside.

2. Fill a blender with the powdered eggs, pickle juice, and homemade mayonnaise. Process until evenly combined and smooth.

3. Pour the creamy dressing over the shrimp.

4. Serve and enjoy.

Cucumber Yogurt Shrimp

Ingredients:

- Lemon juice, freshly squeezed (3 tablespoons)

- Cucumbers, medium, peeled, seeded, diced (2 pieces)

- Dill, chopped finely (1 tablespoon)

- Greek yogurt, plain, fat free (3 cups)

- Garlic, chopped (1 clove)

- Salt (1 tablespoon + a dash)

- Pepper, freshly cracked (a dash)

- Shrimp, large, shelled, deveined, poached (4 ounces)

Directions:

1. After peeling the cucumbers, slice into lengthwise halves. Scrape out the flesh with a spoon before discarding the seeds.

2. Chop the cucumber flesh into cubes, then place in the

colander. Combine with salt (1 tablespoon) and let sit for half an hour.

3. After draining the cucumber pieces, wipe dry with paper towels and place inside the food processor.

4. Pour lemon juice into the food processor. Add in the black pepper, garlic, and dill as well. Process until the mixture is well-blended and smooth, then transfer into a large bowl.

5. Add in the yogurt. Stir to combine. Refrigerate for two to five hours or until all the flavors are blended.

6. Set the poached shrimp on a serving platter.

7. Remove the cucumber yogurt mixture from the refrigerator and pour over the shrimp.

8. Serve and enjoy.

Honey-Glazed Shrimp with Avocado-Strawberry Salad

Ingredients:

- Shrimp, large, shelled, deveined (16 ounces)

- Spring lettuce mix, fresh (6 cups)

- Avocado, sliced into cubes (1 piece)

- Cheese, feta/ Gorgonzola, crumbled (4 ounces)

- Strawberries, hulled, sliced (1 pint)

- Red onion, small, sliced thinly (1/4 piece)

- Almonds, sliced, toasted (1/4 cup)

Glaze:

- Honey (1 tablespoon)

- Liquid smoke (1 teaspoon)

- Olive oil, extra virgin (2 tablespoons)

- Lemon juice, freshly squeezed (1 tablespoon)

- Sea salt (1/4 teaspoon)

Dressing:

- Balsamic vinegar (2 tablespoons)

- Dijon mustard (1 teaspoon)

- Sea salt (1/4 teaspoon)

- Black pepper, freshly ground (1/4 teaspoon)

- Olive oil, extra virgin (1/4 cup)

- Honey (1 tablespoon)

- Garlic powder (1/4 teaspoon)

Directions:

1. Pour the honey in a medium bowl. Add the lemon juice, olive oil, salt, and liquid smoke. Stir to combine; set aside.

2. Set the grill on medium-high to preheat.

3. Meanwhile, rinse the shrimp well. Pat dry with paper towels before brushing with olive oil. Arrange on the preheated grill and cook on each side for about four to five minutes.

4. Once the shrimp pieces are done, transfer onto a plate and brush the tops with the prepared glaze.

5. Arrange equal portions of the spring mix among four individual plates. Add the avocado, strawberries and red onion, then top with the sliced almonds and cheese.

6. Meanwhile, pour the ingredients for the dressing in a medium bowl. Stir to combine before pouring over the salad plates.

7. Top each dressed salad with the glazed shrimp and serve immediately.

8. Enjoy.

Pesto Shrimp

Ingredients:

- Shrimp, large, shelled, deveined, poached (4 ounces)

- Garlic cloves, minced (2 pieces)

- Spinach, frozen, thawed, drained well, chopped (10

ounces)

- Basil, fresh (1/3 cup)

- Olive oil, extra virgin (1 tablespoon)

- Water (1/2 cup)

- Cottage cheese, 1-percent (1/3 cup)

- Parmesan cheese, grated (2 tablespoons)

Directions:

1. Fill the blender with the spinach.

2. Add the garlic, basil, cheeses, olive oil, and water.

3. Process until well-combined and smooth.

4. Arrange the shrimp into a mound on a platter. Drench with the pesto.

5. Serve immediately.

Romaine Shrimp Salad

Ingredients:

- Garlic cloves, minced (2 pieces)

- Baby spinach leaves, fresh, whole (3 cups)

- Kalamata olives (1/3 cup)

- Lemon zest, freshly grated (1/2 teaspoon)

- Tomatoes, medium, sliced thinly into wedges (2 pieces)

- Feta cheese, reduced fat (1/4 cup)

- Shrimp, large, fresh/ frozen, peeled, deveined (1 pound)

- Butter, melted (1 tablespoon)

- Sea salt (1/4 teaspoon)

- Romaine lettuce, torn (3 cups)

- Cucumber, medium, peeled, sliced lengthwise into

quarters about ¼-inch thick (1 piece)

- Red onion, chopped (1/4 cup)

Vinaigrette:

- Vinegar, red wine (1 tablespoon)

- Oregano, fresh, chopped (1 tablespoon)

- Agave nectar (1 tablespoon)

- Black pepper, freshly ground (1/4 teaspoon)

- Olive oil, extra virgin (3 tablespoons)

- Lemon juice, freshly squeezed (1 tablespoon)

- Mint, fresh, chopped (1 tablespoon)

- Sea salt (1/2 teaspoon)

Directions:

1. Get the grill ready. Meanwhile, rinse the shrimp before patting dry with several sheets of paper towels.

2. Stir together the butter, garlic, salt, and lemon zest in a large bowl. Add the shrimp and toss with the butter mixture to combine. After seeing to it that the shrimp pieces are evenly coated, cover the bowl and set aside for about thirty minutes.

3. In another large bowl, toss the spinach and romaine with the olives, tomatoes, red onion, and cucumber. Let sit as you continue working on the shrimp.

4. Thread the butter mixture-coated shrimp onto four skewers (8-inch), making sure they are spaced about ¼-inch apart. Cook on the grill for about six to eight minutes or until opaque. Arrange on a platter and set aside.

5. In a medium bowl, combine the ingredients for the vinaigrette. Process with an immersion blender until evenly mixed and smooth.

6. Top the greens on the platter with feta cheese. Add the grilled shrimp before drizzling with the prepared vinaigrette.

7. Serve and enjoy.

Shrimp and Cranberry Stuffing

Ingredients:

- Celery, chopped (1 cup)

- Tarragon, died (1 teaspoon)

- Water chestnuts, whole (1 cup)

- Bread slices, whole wheat, toasted, sliced into one inch cubes (10 pieces)

- Nutmeg, ground (1/8 teaspoon)

- Shrimp, large, shelled, deveined, poached (8 ounces)

- Chicken broth, low sodium (1 cup)

- Onion, chopped (1/2 cup)

- Parsley, fresh, chopped (1/4 cup)

- Paprika (1/2 teaspoon)

- Cranberries, fresh, chopped (1/2 cup)

- Apple, chopped (1 cup)

Directions:

1. Set the oven at 350 degrees to preheat. Meanwhile, use cooking spray to lightly coat a baking dish (2-quart).

2. Heat a large skillet (nonstick) on medium after filling it with the chicken broth.

3. Stir in the onion and celery. Allow the mixture to cook for about five minutes or until the veggies are tender. Turn off the heat, add the poached shrimp, and let the mixture sit.

4. Place the bread cubes in a large mixing bowl. Add the water chestnuts, chopped apples, and cranberries as well as tarragon, nutmeg, parsley, and paprika. Toss to combine before stirring in the onion-celery mixture.

5. Transfer the shrimp and cranberry stuffing into the prepped dish. Cover with foil before placing in the oven.

6. Bake for about twenty minutes, then remove the foil cover. Return to the oven and bake for another ten minutes.

7. Serve right away.

Shrimp Enchilada

Ingredients:

- Shrimp, large, shelled, deveined, poached (2 cups)

- Enchilada/ taco sauce, canned, divided (1 cup)

- Mexican cheese, reduced fat, shredded (1/2 cup)

- Scallions, medium, white + green portions, chopped (6 pieces)

- Pinto beans, canned, drained, rinsed (15 ounces)

- Tortillas, medium, low carb, fat free (4 pieces)

Directions:

1. Set the oven at 350 degrees to preheat. Meanwhile, slightly coat a baking dish (9x13) with nonstick cook-

ing spray.

2. Place the turkey in a large bowl. Add the beans, enchilada/taco sauce (1/2 cup), and scallions. Stir to combine.

3. Add ¼ of the turkey mixture onto each tortilla. Enclose the fillings by folding up the top, bottom, and sides.

4. Arrange the filled tortillas inside the prepped baking dish, making sure to place them with their seam-sides facing down.

5. Top the enchiladas with the remaining enchilada/taco sauce (1/2 cup) before sprinkling on the cheese.

6. Use aluminum foil to cover the dish before placing in the oven to bake. After twenty minutes or once the cheese is all melted and bubbly, remove from the oven and serve immediately.

Shrimp Rolls

Ingredients:

- Basil pesto, homemade (1/4 cup)

- Bread crumbs, panko (2 tablespoons)

- Olive oil, extra virgin (1 tablespoon)

- Garlic cloves, minced (2 pieces)

- Sea salt (1/4 teaspoon)

- Black pepper, freshly ground (1/4 teaspoon)

- Pecans, chopped finely (1/4 cup)

- Lemon zest, freshly grated (1/2 teaspoon)

- Shrimp, large, shelled, deveined (16 ounces)

- Carrot, shredded (1/4 cup)

Directions:

1. Set the oven at 375 degrees to preheat.

2. Meanwhile, use cooking spray (nonstick) to coat a baking dish (11x7). Set aside.

3. Rinse the shrimp, then pat dry with paper towels. Spread basil pesto (1 tablespoon) onto one side before topping with shredded carrot (1 tablespoon). Loosely roll up each shrimp and secure with a toothpick.

4. Place all loosely rolled up shrimp pieces at the bottom of the prepped dish. Brush olive oil on top.

5. Meanwhile, place the panko breadcrumbs in a large bowl. Add the pecans, garlic, pepper, salt, and lemon zest. Mix well before pressing onto the olive oil-brushed surfaces of the shrimp rolls.

6. Place in the oven to bake for about ten to fifteen minutes or until the shrimp is opaque and the crust is browned.

7. Serve immediately.

Spinach with Lemon-Grilled Shrimp

Ingredients:

- Garlic cloves, minced (2 pieces)

- Black pepper, freshly ground (1/4 teaspoon)

- Baby spinach, packed loosely, washed, dried (5 cups)

- Butter, melted (1 tablespoon)

- Milk, half and half, fat free (1/4 cup)

- Pine nuts, toasted (1/4 cup)

- Shrimp, large, shelled, deveined (1/2 pound)

- Lemon zest, freshly grated (1 tablespoon)

- Lemon juice, freshly squeezed (3 tablespoons)

- Salt (1/2 teaspoon)

- Mascarpone cheese (1/4 cup)

- Nutmeg, freshly grated (1/4 teaspoon)

- Parmesan cheese, shaved (1/4 cup)

Directions:

1. Get the grill ready.

2. Meanwhile, pat the shrimp dry after rinsing well. Place inside a large bowl and toss with salt, pepper, garlic, butter, lemon juice, and lemon zest. Cover and set aside for half an hour.

3. Thread the shrimp pieces onto two skewers (8-inch), making sure to leave a quarter inch of space in between each piece. Arrange the skewered shrimp on the grill to cook for about six to eight minutes or until opaque.

4. Meanwhile, pour the milk into a medium bowl. Add the nutmeg and mascarpone and whisk well until evenly combined. Transfer the mascarpone sauce into a large pot.

5. Heat the pot on low. Stir the mascarpone sauce as you add in the spinach. Once the spinach is wilted, pour in some pasta water (2 tablespoons) and allow

the mixture to cook for two more minutes or until the spinach leaves are cooked.

6. After seasoning the spinach mixture with pepper and salt, pour into a serving bowl. Add pine nuts on top, then sprinkle with Parmesan cheese. Finish off by topping everything with the grilled shrimp.

7. Serve and enjoy.

8 - Turkey Recipes

Easy Herbed Turkey

Ingredients:

- Thyme, dried (1 tablespoon)

- Water (1/2 cup)

- Sage, dried (2 teaspoons)

- Parsley, fresh, chopped (2 tablespoons)

- Olive oil, extra virgin (1 tablespoon)

- Turkey, whole, thawed, 15-pounds (1 piece)

Au jus:

- Thyme, dried (1 tablespoon)

- Honey (2 tablespoons)

- Pan drippings, defatted (1 cup)

- Sage, dried (2 teaspoons)

- Parsley, fresh, chopped (2 tablespoons)

- Apple juice (1/2 cup)

Directions:

1. Set the oven at 325 degrees to preheat. Meanwhile, combine the parsley, thyme, and sage in a small bowl; set aside.

2. Discard the turkey's neck and giblets. Use cool water to rinse the turkey thoroughly inside and out, then use paper towels to pat it dry.

3. Gently loosen the neck skin with your fingers before placing the turkey on a roasting pan's rack, making sure to position it breast-side up. Place the herb mixture (1 tablespoon) beneath each breast skin, then rub the turkey's exterior with olive oil and then the rest of the herb mixture.

4. Secure the turkey legs by loosely tying together before placing the turkey in the oven's middle part. Cook for one hour and thirty minutes before tenting with foil. Cook for another two hours or until nicely roasted, with the juices running clear.

5. Once done, take the turkey out of the oven and let sit for twenty minutes.

6. While the turkey juices are settling in the cooling meat, stir half a cup of water into the skillet (heated on medium-high) as you scrape up the remaining browned turkey bits. Pour into a small bowl, leaving one cup of the drippings in the pan. Add the apple juice, honey, sage, parley, and thyme; stir to combine. Reduce heat to medium and simmer the mixture until reduced to half its original volume.

7. Slice the turkey and serve drizzled with the prepared au jus. Enjoy.

Mouthwatering Turkey Turnovers

Ingredients:

- Turkey meat, ground, breast meat part only (1 pound)

- Crescent rolls, reduced fat, refrigerated (24 pieces)

- Onion soup, dry (1 envelope)

- Cheese, 2-percent low fat, shredded (1 cup)

Directions:

1. Set the oven to 350 degrees to preheat. Meanwhile, line a cookie sheet with parchment paper; set aside.

2. Heat a large skillet (nonstick) on medium after misting with cooking spray. Add the meat and dry onion soup. Stir to combine, then cook until the meat is browned and cooked through.

3. Stir in the cheese. Set aside to cool slightly.

4. Separate the rolls before slicing into halves shaped into triangles.

5. Fill each triangle center with the prepared meat mixture, then fold and seal before arranging on the lined cookie sheet.

6. Place in the oven to bake for fifteen minutes.

7. Serve and enjoy.

Slow Cooked Creamy Turkey

Ingredients:

- Soup, cream of mushroom, reduced fat (10 ¾ ounces)

- Chicken stock (1/2 cup)

- Mushrooms, packaged (8 ounces)

- Turkey breast, boneless, skinless (6 pieces)

- Cottage cheese, pureed (1 cup) OR Greek yogurt, plain, nonfat (1 cup)

- Dressing mix, Italian (0.7 ounces)

Directions:

1. Mist cooking spray on a large skillet (nonstick). Heat on medium-high, then add the turkey breasts. Cook on each side for about two to three minutes or until lightly browned.

2. Once the turkey breasts are done, place in the slow cooker (5-quart).

3. Meanwhile, pour the chicken stock and cream of mushroom soup into the skillet, then stir in the

Italian dressing mix and Greek yogurt/cottage cheese. Heat on medium and allow the mixture to cook for two to three minutes as you stir constantly, or until the mixture is well-blended and smooth.

4. Top the slow cooker turkey with the mushrooms, then submerge with the prepared soup mixture. Cover to cook for four hours on low heat.

5. Give the slow cooker turkey mixture a good stir. Serve and enjoy.

Stir-Fried Eggplant and Turkey

Ingredients:

- Mint, fresh, chopped (2 tablespoons)

- Ginger, peeled, chopped (1 tablespoon)

- Bell pepper, red, seeded, julienned (1 piece)

- Soy sauce, low sodium (2 tablespoons)

- Spring onions, white & green parts, chopped coarsely (2 pieces)

- Spring onions, white & green parts, sliced thinly (1 piece)

- Eggplant, small, unpeeled, diced (4 cups)

- Turkey breasts, boneless, skinless, sliced into two-inch-long & half-inch-wide strips (1 pound)

- Basil, fresh, chopped coarsely (1/4 cup)

- Broth/ stock, turkey/ chicken, low sodium (3/4 cup)

- Garlic cloves (2 pieces)

- Olive oil, extra virgin (2 tablespoons)

- Yellow onion, chopped coarsely (1/2 cup)

- Bell pepper, yellow, seeded, julienned (1 piece)

Directions:

1. Fill a blender with the stock (1/4 cup). Add the garlic, ginger, green onions, mint, and basil. Process until just minced, then set aside.

2. Heat a large frying pan (nonstick) on medium-high.

Add olive oil (1 tablespoon), then stir in the yellow onion, bell peppers, and eggplant. Cook for about eight minutes or until the vegetables are nicely sautéed and tender. Place inside a large bowl and keep warm by covering with paper towels.

3. Pour the rest of the olive oil (1 tablespoon) into the pan and heat on medium-high. Stir in the basil mixture; constantly stir for one minute before stirring in the soy sauce and turkey strips as well. Saute for about two minutes or until the meat is opaque and cooked through.

4. Pour in the remaining stock (1/2 cup). Stir and allow to boil before adding back in the eggplant mixture. Stir the entire mixture for about three minutes or until everything is heated through.

5. Pour the stir-fried turkey-eggplant mixture onto a serving dish (warmed). Serve garnished with green onion slices.

6. Enjoy.

Stuffed Turkey Breasts

Ingredients:

- Onion, chopped (1/2 cup)

- Apple, peeled, chopped (1 cup)

- Milk, fat free (1 cup)

- Lemon, sliced into four wedged pieces (1 piece)

- Garlic, minced (1/4 teaspoon)

- Turkey breast halves, large, w/ bones removed, 6-ounces (4 pieces)

- Flour, all purpose (2 tablespoons)

- Raisins, seedless (3 tablespoons)

- Celery, chopped (1/2 cup)

- Bay leaf (1 piece)

- Water chestnuts, chopped (2 tablespoons)

- Olive oil, extra virgin (2 tablespoons)

- Curry powder (1 teaspoon)

Directions:

1. Set the oven at 425 degrees to preheat.

2. Use cooking spray to coat a large baking dish; set aside.

3. Place the raisins in a small bowl. Pour in warm water to cover and allow the raisins to stay submerged until swelling.

4. After misting cooking spray on a large skillet, heat on medium. Add the garlic, onions, bay leaf, and celery; stir and cook for five minutes or until onions are translucent. Discard the bay leaf before stirring in the apples. Let the mixture cook for two more minutes.

5. After draining the raisins, dry by patting with paper towels. Stir into the apple mixture, along with the water chestnuts. Turn off the heat and allow the mixture to cool.

6. Meanwhile, slightly tug at the turkey breast skin to loosen. Insert the apple mixture into the space between the turkey breast and skin.

7. Heat a new skillet on medium. Add the olive oil; once hot, add the stuffed turkey breasts. Cook on each side for about five minutes or until browned and cooked through.

8. Place the browned turkey breasts at the bottom of the prepped baking dish. Cover and place in the oven to bake for about fifteen minutes or until the internal temperature of the meat reaches 165 degrees. Take the dish out of the oven and set aside.

9. Fill a saucepan with the milk. Stir in the flour and curry powder, then heat on medium. Keep stirring for five minutes or until the mixture has thickened, then immediately pour on top of the stuffed turkey pieces.

10. Cover the dish and bake again for about ten minutes before placing the stuffed turkey breasts on individual plates (warmed). Drench the tops with the prepared milk mixture. Add the lemon wedges and serve

right away.

Turkey and Beans

Ingredients:

- Basil, dried (2 teaspoons)

- Navy beans, rinsed, drained (16 ounces)

- Black pepper, freshly cracked (1/4 teaspoon)

- Basil leaves, fresh/ dried (a handful)

- Turkey breast halves, skinless, boneless, sliced into lengthwise cuts (2 pieces)

- Salt (1/4 teaspoon)

- Bell pepper, yellow, diced (1 cup)

- Tomatoes, un-drained, diced (14 ½ ounces)

Directions:

1. Fill a slow cooker with the turkey.

2. Meanwhile, place the beans in a large mixing bowl. Add the tomatoes, bell pepper, basil, and black pepper. Stir to combine.

3. Pour the bean mixture over the slow cooker turkey pieces. Cover and cook on low for four to six hours.

4. Transfer the cooked turkey onto individual plates. Smother with the bean mixture on top and garnish with basil leaves before serving.

5. Enjoy.

Turkey Spaghetti

Ingredients:

- Spaghetti, uncooked, broken up into 1/3-portions, cooked (8 ounces)

- Scallions, chopped (1/2 cup)

- Black pepper, freshly ground (1/8 teaspoon)

- Pimentos, canned, drained, sliced (1/4 cup)

- Flour, all purpose (3 tablespoons)

- Milk, skim, fat free (1/2 cup)

- Parmesan cheese, grated (3 ½ tablespoons)

- Margarine, reduced calorie (1 tablespoon)

- Button mushrooms, sliced (8 ounces)

- Garlic powder (1/4 teaspoon)

- Chicken broth, fat free (1 cup)

- Turkey breasts, skinless, boneless, cooked, cubed (1/2 pound)

- Cooking wine, sherry (2 tablespoons)

Directions:

1. Heat a large saucepan on medium-high before adding the margarine. Once hot and melted, stir in the mushrooms and scallions. Cook for about five minutes or until tender.

2. Place the flour in a large bowl. Add the pepper and

garlic powder; stir to combine. Pour in the milk and broth, then whisk until well-blended.

3. Stir the flour mixture into the saucepan. Stirring frequently, cook for about ten minutes or until the mixture boils and starts thickening.

4. Stir in the pimentos, turkey, and sherry. Cook for about two minutes or until the entire mixture is heated through.

5. Add the cooked spaghetti as well as the cheese. Gently toss to combine, making sure the spaghetti is evenly coated.

6. Serve and enjoy.

Turkey Tacos

Ingredients:

- Taco seasoning mix, dry (1 ¼ ounces)

- Turkey breasts, boneless, skinless (1 pound)

- Chicken broth, low sodium (1 cup)

Directions:

1. Pour the chicken broth in a large bowl. Add the taco seasoning and stir to combine.

2. Fill a slow cooker with the turkey breasts.

3. Add the broth mixture to the slow cooker, ensuring the turkey pieces are evenly covered.

4. Secure the slow cooker lid and allow the turkey to cook for six to eight hours on low heat.

5. Uncover and shred the turkey meat with two forks.

6. Cover again to cook on low for another half hour.

7. Serve as is, on top of your favorite salad, or stuffed into tacos.

8. Enjoy.

Wonderfully Succulent Turkey

Ingredients:

- Bread crumbs, Italian, whole wheat (1 ¼ cups

- Turkey breasts, boneless, skinless (3 pounds)

- Mayonnaise, light (1/2 cup)

Directions:

1. Set the oven to 425 degrees to preheat.

2. Brush all sides of the turkey with the light mayonnaise.

3. Pour the breadcrumbs all over the turkey, pressing lightly to ensure they adhere well.

4. Line a baking pan with foil. Add the coated turkey and place in the oven.

5. Bake for about forty to forty-five minutes or until the internal temperature of the meat reaches 165 degrees.

6. Serve immediately.

9 - Pork & Beef Recipes

Beefy Brown Rice and Black Bean Casserole

Ingredients:

- Swiss cheese, low fat, shredded (2 cups)

- Vegetable broth, low sodium (1 cup)

- Ground beef (1 pound)

- Black beans, drained (15 ounces)

- Onion, diced (1/3 cup)

- Cumin (1/2 teaspoon)

- Carrots, shredded (1/3 cup)

- Brown rice (1/3 cup)

- Olive oil, extra virgin (1 tablespoon)

- Zucchini, medium, sliced thinly (1 piece)

- Mushrooms, sliced (1/2 cup)

- Cayenne pepper (1/4 teaspoon)

- Green chilies, diced (4 ounces)

Directions:

1. Pour the vegetable broth into a large pot. Add the rice and stir, then allow the mixture to boil. Turn heat down to low before covering the pot and letting the rice mixture simmer for about forty-five minutes or until tender.

2. Meanwhile, set the oven at 350 degrees to preheat.

3. Use cooking spray (nonstick) to mist a casserole dish (large) until well-greased. Set aside.

4. Heat a large skillet on medium before adding in the olive oil. Stir in the onions and cook for two minutes or until tender and fragrant.

5. Add the seasonings as well as zucchini, mushrooms, and ground beef into the pan. Stir to combine and cook for another two to three minutes or until the zucchini is lightly caramelized and the entire mixture

is heated through. Turn off the heat and set aside.

6. Transfer the cooked rice into a large bowl. Add the beef mixture as well as the beans, carrots, Swiss cheese (1 cup), and chilies. Toss to combine, then pour into the greased casserole dish.

7. Top with the remaining Swiss cheese (1 cup), then cover loosely with foil. Place in the oven to bake for half an hour.

8. Remove the dish from the oven. Uncover and return to the oven to bake for another ten minutes or until the surface is lightly browned.

9. Serve immediately.

Delicious Asian Style Pork Tenderloin

Ingredients:

- Brown sugar (1/3 cup)

- Mustard, dry (1 tablespoon)

- Garlic cloves, minced (4 pieces)

- Lemon juice, freshly squeezed (2 tablespoons)

- Pepper, freshly cracked (1 ½ teaspoons)

- Soy sauce, light (1/3 cup)

- Worcestershire sauce (2 tablespoons)

- Rice vinegar (2 tablespoons)

- Ginger (1 tablespoon)

- Pork tenderloin (2 pounds)

Directions:

1. Fill a large plastic bag (freezer-safe) with all the ingredients, except the pork tenderloin.

2. Toss the bag contents until well-combined.

3. Add the pork tenderloin and gently rub with the marinade.

4. Seal the bag and place in the refrigerator to marinate overnight.

5. Remove the bag from the refrigerator; place in the oven, preheated at 375 degrees), to bake for thirty to forty minutes. (Alternatively, cook on low in the slow cooker for four to six hours.)

6. Pour into a serving bowl and serve immediately.

Easy Chili

Ingredients:

- Onion, chopped (1/2 cup)

- Jalapeno peppers, seeded, chopped (1/2 teaspoon)

- Sugar (1 teaspoon)

- Kidney beans, canned, rinsed, drained (4 cups)

- Cornmeal (2 tablespoons)

- Tomatoes, large (2 pieces)

- Celery, chopped (1 cup)

- Chili powder (1 ½ tablespoons)

- Water (as needed)

Directions:

1. Heat a soup pot on medium. Add the onion and ground beef, then sauté for two to three minutes or until the onion turns translucent and the meat is browned and cooked.

2. Drain the beef mixture before adding the celery, chili powder, sugar, kidney beans, and tomatoes. Stir to combine, then cover to cook for about ten minutes.

3. Stir in water and cornmeal. Allow the mixture to cook for ten to fifteen more minutes or until all the flavors are well-blended.

4. Transfer the chili into individual bowls (warmed). Top with jalapeno peppers before serving right away.

5. Enjoy.

Faux Fried Pork Tenderloin

Ingredients:

- Paprika (1/8 teaspoon)

- Soup mix, onion, dry (1 tablespoon)

- Bran cereal (1/3 cup)

- Salt, kosher (1/4 teaspoon)

- Buttermilk, reduced fat (1/3 cup)

- Pork tenderloin, raw, 1 1/4-inches each (10 pieces)

- Breadcrumbs, panko (1/3 cup)

Directions:

1. Pour the buttermilk into a large Ziploc bag. Add the paprika and combine well before adding in the chicken. Make sure the chicken is completely coated. Seal and place in the refrigerator for a minimum of one hour.

2. Set the oven at 375 degrees to preheat. Meanwhile, use cooking spray to coat a baking sheet (large).

3. Pour the cereal into the blender. Process until ground

to a breadcrumb-texture. Transfer into a large mixing bowl. Add the onion soup mix as well as panko breadcrumbs. Stir to combine.

4. Take the chicken pieces out of the buttermilk bag and dredge in the breadcrumb mixture. Arrange on the prepped baking sheet and place in the preheated oven.

5. Bake for about ten minutes before flipping to cook on the other side for another ten minutes or until crispy and completely cooked. .

6. Serve and enjoy.

Pork Tenderloin and Apple Cider Curry

Ingredients:

- Curry powder (1 ½ tablespoons)

- Apple, tart, peeled, seeded, sliced into one inch cubes (1 piece)

- Yellow onions, medium, chopped (2 cups)

- Cornstarch (1 tablespoon)

- Pork tenderloin, sliced into 6 portions (16 ounces)

- Olive oil, extra virgin (1 tablespoon)

- Apple cider, divided (2 cups)

Directions:

1. Rub the curry powder onto all surfaces of the pork tenderloin; let sit for fifteen minutes.

2. Meanwhile, heat a large skillet (heavy bottomed) on medium-high before adding the olive oil. Add the seasoned pork tenderloin and cook for five minutes on each side or until browned and cooked through. Transfer onto a plate and let sit to cool.

3. Fill the same skillet with the onions. Stir and cook for two minutes or until golden and softened. Pour in the apple cider (1 ½ cups); stir to combine and turn the heat down to medium-low. Allow the mixture to simmer until reduced to ½ its original volume.

4. Stir in the cornstarch, remaining apple cider (1/2

cup), and the apple cubes. Let the mixture simmer for two minutes or until thickened, then add the cooked pork tenderloin. Let the mixture simmer again for five minutes before removing from the heat.

5. Transfer the pork tenderloin onto a platter. Drench with the sauce.

6. Serve and enjoy.

Stir-Fried Ginger Beef

Ingredients:

- Water chestnuts, sliced (8 ounces)

- Garlic cloves, medium (2 pieces)

- Cornstarch (1 tablespoon)

- Bell pepper, medium, green/ red/ yellow, sliced into strips (1/2 piece)

- Hoisin sauce (2 ounces)

- Red pepper flakes, crushed (1/4 teaspoon)

- Bok choy stalks, medium, sliced into half inch strips (2 pieces)

- Flank steak, sliced into quarter-inch strips (1 pound)

- Beef broth, fat free (6 ounces)

- Canola oil (1 teaspoon)

- Broccoli florets (3 ounces)

- Brown rice, instant (1/2 cup)

Directions:

1. Place the steak in a large bowl. Add the ginger and garlic, then toss to combine. Let sit while you work on the rice.

2. Follow package directions in cooking the rice.

3. Meanwhile, fill a medium bowl with the broth. Add the cornstarch, soy sauce, and hoisin sauce. Stir to combine, making sure the cornstarch is completely dissolved. Set aside.

4. Heat a large skillet on medium-high. Add the oil, then stir in the red pepper flakes. Add the steak and cook for two to three minutes on each side or until browned and cooked through. Remove from heat and set aside.

5. Add the bell pepper, carrot, and broccoli to the same skillet. Cook for about two to three minutes or until nicely crisp yet tender.

6. Add the water chestnuts and bok choy; stir and cook for two more minutes or until the bok choy is crisp but still tender.

7. Create a well in the skillet mixture's center, then fill with the broth. Stirring occasionally, let the north cook for one to two minutes or until thickened.

8. Stir in the beef and cook for one to two minutes or until heated through.

9. Pour your stir-fried ginger beef over rice and serve right away.

10. Enjoy.

Slow Cooker Beef with Brown Rice

Ingredients:

- Onion, large, diced (1 piece)

- Greek yogurt, plain (1 ½ cups)

- Paprika (1/2 tablespoon)

- Bay leaves (2 pieces)

- Ginger, fresh, minced (2 tablespoons)

- Garam masala (2 tablespoons)

- Black pepper, freshly ground (3/4 teaspoon)

- Cilantro, fresh, chopped (a handful)

- Ground beef (3 pounds)

- Garlic cloves, minced (4 pieces)

- Tomato puree (29 ounces)

- Olive oil, extra virgin (2 tablespoons)

- Cumin (1 tablespoon)

- Cinnamon (3/4 teaspoon)

- Cayenne pepper (2 teaspoons)

- Brown rice, cooked

Directions:

1. Fill a large bowl with all the ingredients, except for the chicken and bay leaves.

2. Stir to combine before adding the chicken. Stir again to coat the chicken thoroughly.

3. Transfer the chicken mixture to the slow cooker. Top with the bay leaves before covering.

4. Cook for four hours on high or eight hours on low.

5. After discarding the bay leaves, top with the cilantro and serve over brown rice.

Tart 'n Sweet Pork

Ingredients:

- Pineapple chunks, canned, unsweetened (15 ounces)

- Table salt (1/2 teaspoon)

- Brown rice, cooked (3 cups)

- Splenda (1/4 cup)

- Green peppers, medium, sliced (2 pieces)

- Pork tenderloin lean, sliced thinly into strips (1 pound)

- Water (1/2 cup)

- Onion, small, sliced (1 piece)

- Wine vinegar (1/3 cup)

- Cornstarch (2 tablespoons)

- Soy sauce, low sodium (1 tablespoon)

Directions:

1. Heat a large skillet (nonstick) on medium-high after generously coating with cooking spray.

2. Stir in the pork strips; cook for about four to five minutes or until golden brown. Once done, transfer onto a plate and let sit. Discard any remaining skillet fat.

3. Meanwhile, drain the pineapple chunks, setting aside the juice in a medium bowl. Add the water, soy sauce, vinegar, cornstarch, sugar, and salt. Stir to combine before adding to the skillet. Allow the mixture to cook for about two minutes or until thickened.

4. Stir in the cooked pork strips and reduce heat to low. Cook for another thirty minutes or until the meat has tenderized.

5. Stir in the drained pineapple chunks as well as onion and peppers. Allow the mixture to cook for five more minutes or until heated through.

6. Pour on top of cooked brown rice.

7. Serve and enjoy.

10 - Veggie Recipes

Baked Broccoli and Eggs

Ingredients:

- Margarine, light (4 ounces)

- Broccoli, frozen, thawed, chopped (10 ounces)

- Pimento, jarred, chopped (4 ounces)

- Flour (6 tablespoons)

- Black pepper, freshly ground (1 dash)

- Mushrooms, sliced, fresh (1/2 cup)

- Eggs, large (6 pieces)

- Cheddar cheese, low fat (1/2 pound)

- Cottage cheese, nonfat (2 pounds)

- Salt (1 teaspoon)

- Paprika (1 dash)

Directions:

1. Set the oven to 350 degrees to preheat.

2. Meanwhile, place the eggs, broccoli, and all other ingredients in a large bowl. Stir to combine.

3. Use cooking spray to coat the sides and bottom of a casserole dish (2-quart).

4. Fill the prepped dish with the broccoli-egg mixture, making sure to spread it evenly.

5. Bake in the oven for one hour and thirty minutes.

6. Serve immediately.

Black Bean and Pumpkin Soup

Ingredients:

- Onion, medium, chopped (1 piece)

- Black pepper, freshly ground (1/2 teaspoon)

- Pumpkin puree, canned (16 ounces)

- Cumin, ground (1 tablespoon)

- Tomatoes, canned, diced (1 cup)

- Olive oil, extra virgin (2 tablespoons)

- Garlic cloves, minced (4 pieces)

- Chili powder (1 teaspoon)

- Black beans, canned, rinsed, drained (30 ounces)

- Beef broth, low sodium (2 cups)

Directions:

1. Heat a soup kettle on medium after filling with the oil.

2. Add the garlic, onions, pepper, chili powder, and cumin. Stir and cook for about two to three minutes or until soft and fragrant.

3. Add the broth as well as pumpkin, tomatoes, and black beans. Stir to combine.

4. Allow the mixture to simmer, uncovered, for twenty-five minutes or until thickened to your desired con-

sistency.

5. Remove from heat and process the black bean and pumpkin soup with an immersion blender.

6. Serve and enjoy.

Broccoli and Tofu Quiche

Ingredients:

- Salt (1/4 teaspoon)

- Mushrooms, chopped (1/4 pound)

- Pickled plum/ white miso paste (1 tablespoon)

- Yellow onion, chopped (1 piece)

- Sesame tahini (2 tablespoons)

- Bulgur wheat, uncooked (1/2 cup)

- Sesame oil (1 tablespoon)

- Broccoli, chopped (1/2 pound)

- Tofu (1 ½ pounds)

- Tamari (1 tablespoon)

Directions:

1. Set the oven at 350 degrees to preheat.

2. Fill a small pot with water (1 cup) and heat on medium. Bring to a boil before adding in the bulgur and salt. Stir to combine and allow the mixture to boil again.

3. Reduce heat to low and cover to cook for about fifteen minutes. Meanwhile, grease a pie pan (9-inch) with a little oil.

4. Pour the cooked bulgur into the pie pan, pressing lightly to spread it evenly at the bottom. Place in the oven to bake for about twelve minutes or until crusty on top. Let stand to cool.

5. Heat a large skillet (nonstick) on medium-high before adding the onions. Stir in the mushrooms and broccoli and cook for two minutes. Cover and immedi-

ately remove from heat.

6. Meanwhile, fill the food processor with the tofu. Add the tamari, tahini, and umeboshi paste. Process until well-combined and smooth, then pour into a large bowl. Add the cooked veggies and gently toss until evenly coated.

7. Transfer the veggie mixture onto the crusted bulgur. Bake in the oven for about half an hour. Once done, let stand on a wire rack.

8. After ten minutes, slice into 6 portions and serve immediately.

Cheese-Filled Acorn Squash

Ingredients:

- Tofu, firm (1 pound)

- Basil (1 teaspoon)

- Black pepper, freshly ground (1 pinch)

- Onion, chopped finely (1 teaspoon)

- Garlic powder (1 teaspoon)

- Cheddar cheese, reduced fat, shredded (1 cup)

- Acorn squash, halved, seeded (2 pieces)

- Celery, diced (1 cup)

- Mushrooms, fresh, sliced (1 cup)

- Oregano (1 teaspoon)

- Salt (1/8 teaspoon)

- Tomato sauce (8 ounces)

Directions:

1. Set the oven at 350 degrees to preheat.

2. Arrange the acorn squash pieces, with their cut-sides facing down, at the bottom of a glass dish.

3. Place in the microwave oven and cook for about twenty minutes or until softened. Set aside.

4. Heat a saucepan (nonstick) on medium, then add the

tofu (sliced into cubes). Cook until browned before stirring in the onion and celery. Cook for two minutes or until the onion is translucent.

5. Add the mushrooms. Stir to combine and cook for an additional two to three minutes. Pour in the tomato sauce as well as the dry seasonings.

6. Give everything a good stir, then spoon equal portions of the mixture inside the acorn squash pieces.

7. Cover and place in the oven to cook for about fifteen minutes. Uncover and top with the cheese before returning to the oven. Cook for five more minutes or until the cheese is melted and bubbling.

8. Serve immediately.

Cheesy Spinach Bake

Ingredients:

- Eggs, whole (2 pieces)

- Parmesan cheese (1/2 cup)

- Cottage cheese, fat-free/ low fat (2 cups)

- Spinach, frozen, thawed, drained (10 ounces)

Directions:

1. Set the oven to 350 degrees to preheat. Meanwhile, line a baking pan (8x8) with parchment paper.

2. Place all ingredients in a large bowl. Stir to combine.

3. Pour the cheesy spinach mixture into the prepped pan.

4. Place in the oven to bake for twenty to thirty minutes or until the cheese on top is bubbling.

5. Remove from the oven and allow to cool for five minutes.

6. Serve sprinkled with garlic, salt, and pepper.

7. Enjoy.

Mushroom and Wild Rice Soup

Ingredients:

- Onion, white, chopped (1/2 piece)

- White wine (1/2 cup) OR chicken broth, fat free, low sodium (1/2 cup)

- Thyme, dried (1/4 teaspoon)

- Carrots, chopped (1/4 cup)

- Milk, half and half, fat free (1 cup)

- Wild rice, cooked (1 cup)

- Olive oil, extra virgin (1 tablespoon)

- Celery, chopped (1/4 cup)

- White mushrooms, fresh, sliced (1 ½ cups)

- Chicken broth, fat free, low sodium (2 ½ cups)

- Flour (2 tablespoons)

- Black pepper, freshly ground (1/2 teaspoon)

Directions:

1. Heat a stock pot on medium, then add the olive oil.

2. Stir in the chopped onion as well as carrots and celery. Cook for two to three minutes or until tender and fragrant.

3. Pour in the chicken broth and white wine. Add the mushrooms as well, then stir to combine. Cover and allow the mixture to get heated through.

4. Meanwhile, place the flour in a large bowl. Add the milk, pepper, and thyme; stir to combine. Add the cooked rice and toss until well-combined.

5. Transfer the rice mixture into the vegetable pot. Stir well before cooking on medium until bubbly and thickened.

6. Serve immediately.

Mushroom and Zucchini Boats

Ingredients:

- Mushrooms, button, sliced (1 pound)

- Tomato, large, diced (1 piece)

- Pepper, freshly cracked (1/4 teaspoon)

- Egg, beaten (1 piece)

- Breadcrumbs, whole wheat, seasoned (1/4 cup)

- Mozzarella cheese, low fat, shredded (1 cup)

- Zucchini, medium (4 pieces)

- Onion, chopped (1/2 cup)

- Mushrooms, sliced (1/2 pound)

- Spaghetti sauce (3/4 cup)

- Salt, kosher (1/4 teaspoon)

Directions:

1. Set the oven at 350 degrees to preheat.

2. Slice the zucchini into lengthwise halves, then chop a thin slice off the zucchini bottoms so they can sit flat. Remove the pulp and place in a large bowl; set aside.

3. Meanwhile, arrange the empty quarter-inch shells at the bottom of a microwave-safe dish (3-quart, ungreased). Cover before placing in the microwave; heat on high for three minutes or until the shells are crisp and tender. Drain well before setting aside on a plate.

4. Heat a large skillet on medium. Add the onion and mushrooms, stir well, and cook for five minutes or until tender. Turn off the heat and set aside.

5. To the bowl containing the zucchini pulp, add the breadcrumbs, cheese (1/2 cup), spaghetti sauce, tomato, pepper, salt, beaten egg, and the cooked mushrooms. Toss gently to combine.

6. Fill each zucchini shell with the mushroom mixture (1/4 cup), then top with the rest of the cheese. Place in the preheated oven to bake for about twenty minutes or until browned on top.

7. Serve and enjoy.

Nom Nom Veggie Burger

Ingredients:

- Mustard (1 tablespoon)

- Hamburger bun, whole wheat (1 piece)

- Ketchup, homemade (1 tablespoon)

- Burger, mozzarella flavored (1 piece)

- Mayonnaise, homemade (1 tablespoon)

- Tomato slices

- Lettuce leaves

- Onion slices

Directions:

1. Follow package directions in cooking the mozzarella flavored burger.

2. Top the hamburger bun with the cooked veggie burger.

3. Finish the burger by topping with the homemade mayonnaise and ketchup, lettuce leaves, and tomato and onion slices.

4. Serve and enjoy.

Quick Spinach Frittata

Ingredients:

- Onion, medium chopped (1 piece)

- Eggs, whole (2 pieces)

- Nutmeg (1/8 teaspoon)

- Cheddar cheese, reduced fat, shredded (1 ½ cups)

- Cayenne pepper (1/4 teaspoon)

- Vegetable oil (2 teaspoons)

- Spinach, frozen, thawed, drained, chopped (10 ounces)

- Egg whites (4 pieces)

- Cottage cheese, reduced fat (1/3 cup)

- Salt (1/8 teaspoon)

Directions:

1. Set the oven at 375 degrees to preheat. Meanwhile, use oil spray (vegetable) to coat a pie pan (9-inch).

2. Heat a medium-size skillet over medium-high heat. Add the oil; once heated through, stir in the onion. Cook for about five minutes or until the onion is softened.

3. Stir in the spinach. Let the mixture cook for another three minutes before setting aside.

4. Meanwhile, fill the bottom of the pie pan with cheese before topping with the spinach mixture.

5. Place the whole eggs in a large bowl. Add the egg whites as well as cottage cheese, nutmeg, salt, and cayenne pepper. Stir to combine and pour on top of the cheese and spinach layers.

6. Place in the oven to bake for thirty to thirty-five minutes or until set.

7. Let cool for five minutes before slicing into wedges.

8. Serve and enjoy.

Vegetarian Chili and Cheese

Ingredients:

- Olive oil, extra virgin (2 teaspoons)

- Tomatoes, canned, diced (14 ½ ounces) OR fresh (2 cups)

- Red kidney beans, canned, rinsed (30 ounces)

- Onion, chopped (1 cup)

- Chili powder (2 tablespoons)

- Cheddar cheese, low fat, shredded (1 cup)

- Garlic cloves (2 pieces)

- Green bell pepper, large, diced (1 piece)

- Mushrooms, sliced (1/2 pound)

- Tomato sauce (8 ounces)

- Zucchini, medium, sliced thinly (1 piece)

- Corn, frozen (10 ounces)

Directions:

1. Heat a large skillet on medium-high before adding the olive oil.

2. Stir in the onions as well as mushrooms and green pepper. Cook for two to three minutes or until tender and fragrant.

3. Pour in the tomato sauce along with the chili powder and diced tomatoes. Stir well before allowing the mixture to boil.

4. Reduce heat to low and then stir in the kidney beans and zucchini. Simmer the mixture for about ten to fifteen minutes.

5. Stir in the cheddar cheese (1/2 cup) and frozen corn before letting the mixture simmer for another ten to fifteen minutes.

6. Top with the remaining cheddar cheese and serve

right away.

11 - Snacks & Treats Recipes

Apple and Squash Bake

Ingredients:

- Apples, medium, peeled, cored, sliced thinly into wedges (2 pieces)

- Flour, all purpose (1 tablespoon)

- Salt (1/3 teaspoon)

- Butternut squash, medium, peeled, sliced into ¾-inch cubed pieces (1 piece)

- Splenda (1 tablespoon)

- Butter, melted (1/4 cup)

- Cinnamon, ground (2 teaspoons)

Directions:

1. Fill a casserole dish with the apples and squash. Stir together until combined.

2. Place the rest of the ingredients in a medium bowl.

Stir to combine and pour on top of the apple-squash mixture. Give everything a good stir before covering with foil.

3. Place in the oven to bake for about fifty minutes or until tender.

4. Remove the foil and cook for another ten minutes or until crispy on top.

5. Serve and enjoy.

Cheesy Fluffs

Ingredients:

- Whipped topping, sugar-free (8 ounces)

- Cottage cheese, fat-free (48 ounces)

- Gelatin, sugar-free, flavored (6 ounces)

Directions:

1. Place the whipped topping, cottage cheese and gelatin in a large bowl.

2. Stir until well-combined.

3. Serve topped with blueberries and enjoy.

Chicken and Cheese Quiche

Ingredients:

- Chicken breast, grilled, sliced into one-inch cubes (6 ounces)

- Eggs, large (3 pieces)

- Oregano (1/8 teaspoon)

- Swiss cheese, low fat, sliced into cubes (4 ounces)

- Mozzarella cheese, low fat, shredded (10 ounces)

- Milk, skim (1 cup)

Directions:

1. Set the oven to 400 degrees to preheat.

2. Meanwhile, use cooking spray (nonstick) to lightly coat a pie pan. Fill with the chicken breast and Swiss

cheese cubes, making sure they evenly cover the bottom of the pan. Top with the shredded mozzarella before sprinkling with oregano.

3. Pour the skim milk and eggs into a large bowl. Whip until well-combined and smooth, then pour on top of the chicken-cheese mixture.

4. Place in the oven to bake for about forty minutes or until lightly brown on top.

5. Remove from the oven and allow to slightly cool.

6. Serve and enjoy right away.

Deliciously Spicy Deviled Eggs

Ingredients:

- Egg whites, hard boiled (6 pieces)

- Egg yolks, hard boiled (3 pieces)

- Dill (1/2 teaspoon)

- Salt (1/8 teaspoon)

- Horseradish sauce, creamy (2 tablespoons) OR Greek yogurt, plain (2 tablespoons)

- Mustard, spicy (1/4 teaspoon)

- Paprika (1/4 teaspoon)

- Black pepper, freshly ground (1/4 teaspoon)

Directions:

1. Remove the peel off each egg before slicing into lengthwise halves.

2. Pour 3 egg yolks into a large bowl (reserve the egg whites and the remaining three yolks).

3. Add the Greek yogurt/ horseradish sauce as well as salt, dill, and mustard. Whisk to combine.

4. Fill each halved egg white with the egg filling, then sprinkle with the paprika and pepper.

5. Serve and enjoy.

Dreamy Pumpkin Mousse

Ingredients:

- Vanilla pudding, fat-free (4 ounces)

- Milk, skim (1/2 cup)

- Splenda (1/4 teaspoon)

- Ginger, minced (1/4 teaspoon)

- Allspice (1/4 teaspoon)

- Clove (1/4 teaspoon)

- Nutmeg (1/4 teaspoon)

- Pumpkin, canned (15 ounces)

- Whipped topping, sugar-free (2 cups)

- Cinnamon (1 teaspoon)

Directions:

1. Place all ingredients in a large bowl.

2. Whisk until well-combined and evenly smooth.

3. Serve and enjoy.

Egg Enchilada

Ingredients:

- Black pepper, freshly ground (1/4 teaspoon)

- Salsa (2 tablespoons)

- Greek yogurt, fat-free, plain (2 tablespoons)

- Egg, whole (1 piece)

- Egg white (1 piece)

- Tofu (1 ounce)

- Cheese, Mexican blend, shredded (1 tablespoon)

Directions:

1. Place the egg as well as egg white in a medium bowl. Whip together until scrambled.

2. Heat a skillet (nonstick) on medium after coating its bottom with cooking spray.

3. Add the scrambled egg mixture and spread into a round shape. Cook without stirring for one to two minutes or until firm on the edges. Sprinkle on salt and black pepper before flipping to the other side. Cook for another one to two minutes or until cooked through.

4. Slide the cooked egg onto a plate. Add the tofu and cheese, then roll up.

5. Serve your egg enchilada topped with Greek yogurt and salsa.

6. Enjoy right away.

French Toast Sandwiches

Ingredients:

- Ricotta cheese, fat-free (1/2 cup)

- Egg whites (3 pieces)

- Pumpkin pie spice (1/4 teaspoon)

- Bread slices, reduced calorie (4 pieces)

- Stevia (2 packets)

- Salt (1/4 teaspoon)

- Vanilla (1/4 teaspoon)

Directions:

1. Top each slice of bread with equal portions of the ricotta. Sprinkle inthe sugar substitute (1 packet per bread slice). Top with the remaining bread slices. Set aside.

2. Meanwhile, place the egg whites in a medium bowl. Beat until combined, then stir in the salt, vanilla, and pumpkin pie spice.

3. Heat a nonstick skillet (coated with cooking spray) on medium. Coat each sandwich in the egg white mixture, then add to the heated skillet. Cook for five minutes or until browned on each side.

4. Serve and enjoy.

Power Pancakes

Ingredients:

- Baking soda (1/2 teaspoon)

- Canola oil (1/2 tablespoon)

- Flour, all-purpose (1/3 cup)

- Cottage cheese, low fat (1 cup)

- Eggs, beaten lightly (3 pieces)

Directions:

1. Fill a medium bowl with the baking soda and flour. Stir to combine and set aside.

2. Fill a large bowl with the rest of the ingredients. Stir to combine before adding the flour mixture. Keep stirring until the flour mixture is incorporated into the cheese mixture.

3. Meanwhile, heat a large skillet on medium after

lightly coating with cooking spray. Add the prepared batter in batches and cook for two minutes or until bubbling on the surface. Flip to cook the top sides for one minute or until browned.

4. Pour in some syrup (low-calorie) and serve right away.

5. Enjoy.

Turkey-Stuffed Cabbage Rolls

Ingredients:

- Brown rice (1/3 cup)

- Ground turkey, 93-percent lean (1 pound)

- Tomato sauce (2 cups)

- Onion, medium, diced (1/2 piece)

- Oregano/ Italian seasoning (2 teaspoons)

- Cabbage head, w/ individual leaves removed (1 piece)

- Olive oil, extra virgin (1 teaspoon)

- Carrots, medium, diced (2 pieces)

- Garlic powder (2 teaspoons)

Directions:

1. Set the oven at 350 degrees to preheat.

2. After washing the cabbage leaves, blanch for half a minute and set aside in a medium bowl.

3. Follow package directions in cooking the rice.

4. In the meantime, heat a large skillet on medium before adding the olive oil. Stir in the onions as well as carrots; cook for three to four minutes or until softened and caramelized.

5. Stir in the turkey and cook for ten minutes or until browned and cooked through.

6. Stir in the seasonings as well as powders, then add the cooked rice. Toss gently to combine.

7. Fill the center of each cabbage leaf with half a cup of the turkey-rice mixture. Roll up and seal the edges

before placing in the baking dish, making sure their seams are facing down.

8. Smother the cabbage rolls with tomato sauce and place in the preheated oven. Bake for about thirty-five to forty-five minutes or until done.

9. Remove from the oven and let stand to cool.

10. Serve after five to ten minutes.

Book 1 - Gastric Sleeve Cookbook

Effortless Guide To Survive And Thrive Post-Surgery (Weight Loss Surgery Tips, Bariatric, Roux-en-Y, Sleeve Diet, Emotional Support)

1 - Introduction

I want to thank you and congratulate you for buying this book.

This book contains proven steps and strategies on how to understand what you will go through after undergoing gastric sleeve surgery. It helps to prepare you for the emotional, psychological, and physical challenges that you will face as you journey towards losing weight. It also sheds light on the common nutrition complications and how you can cope with them.

This book explains the diet phases that you have to religiously follow before and after the surgery. It provides ample recipes that you can prepare after you have fully recovered and are ready to adapt to a healthier lifestyle with stricter food choices. Remember that the surgery is a life-altering procedure. It prompts you to lead a healthier lifestyle in order to lose weight and maintain your ideal figure.

Thanks again for buying this book, I hope you enjoy it!

2 - An Overview of the Gastric Sleeve Surgery

Bariatric surgery is an effective weight loss technique, which also lowers your risk of various health ailments associated with obesity. It works in two ways: malabsorption and restriction. Malabsorption happens as a result of the bypass of a portion of your small intestine.

As a result, your body will get a minimal amount of nutrients and calories. Restriction happens as the number of calories that you eat becomes limited. The operation works by physically limiting the amount of food that your stomach can take.

There are 4 common types of weight-loss surgery:

Laparoscopic adjustable gastric banding

During the surgery, a band that has an inflatable balloon is fixed in the upper area of the stomach. It becomes a small stomach pouch located at the upper part of the band with a small opening to the stomach. A port is also inserted beneath the skin of the abdomen, which is connected to the band via a tube.

The balloon can be inflated or deflated by removing the fluid through the port. This makes it possible to adjust the size of the band. The process limits the amount of food that the stomach can carry. It makes you feel full sooner but your body is still able to absorb the right amount of nutrients and calories.

Biliopancreatic diversion with duodenal switch

The process removes a large part of the stomach. The surgeon retains the duodenum or the first part of the small intestine and the valve responsible for the food discharge to the small intestine. The duodenal switch is performed by closing the center part of the small intestine and the last part is attached to the duodenum.

The part of the intestine that is separated is then reattached to the rear portion of the intestine. This allows the biliopancreatic diversion or when that portion of the intestine receives the flow of pancreatic digestive juices and bile.

The changes result in the limited nutrients and calories absorption since the food bypasses most parts of the small intestine. This factor along with the smaller size of your stomach will result in weight loss.

Roux-en-Y gastric bypass

In this process, a small pouch is created at the upper portion of the stomach. The pouch is the only area where food can go through. This means that you will have a greater limit of the amount of food and drinks that you can comfortably take at a time. The small intestine is trimmed near the bottom part of the stomach and connected to the pouch.

As a result, the main portion of the stomach continues to process digestive juices as the food travels from the pouch to the small intestine. The surgeon makes connections so that the digestive juices also flow through the small intestine. This setup limits the calories and nutrients absorbed by the body.

Sleeve gastrectomy

Similar to the biliopancreatic diversion, this process separates and removes a part of the stomach from the body. The remaining portion of the tummy is transformed into a structure that looks like a tube. Since the stomach is smaller, it can only hold a limited amount of food.

The process also causes a limited production of ghrelin, an appetite-regulating hormone. This makes you crave less for food. Unlike the biliopancreatic diversion though, this process doesn't limit the absorption of the nutrients and calories.

3 - More about the Gastric Sleeve Surgery

Gastric sleeve or sleeve gastrectomy is becoming the most preferred method among the other weight loss surgeries. It is faster and has a lower risk of complications. Other than these, gastric sleeve offers the following advantages over the other methods:

1. You will have a reduced appetite and less cravings for food.

2. The procedure is laparoscopic, which is less invasive since it only requires small abdominal incisions.

3. It doesn't involve a bypass. The digestive system will not experience rerouting, unlike the other methods. After the process, the stomach will continue to function as usual but since it is smaller, you will feel full sooner.

4. There are patients who don't qualify for gastric bypass surgery that are allowed to undergo gastric sleeve surgery. These are the patients who have a history or are suffering from certain health problems

that include Crohn's disease and anemia.

5. It takes a shorter period to finish the procedure. The surgery takes an hour or so, which makes the amount of time under anesthesia shorter. The hospital stay is also shorter at around 1 to 2 days.

6. It has fewer complications than the other weight loss surgeries.

7. The process is irreversible but if you experience a stall in weight loss, it can be converted to a gastric by-pass 6 to 18 months after the procedure.

8. Nothing needs to be realigned after the process since there are no foreign objects inserted into your body. This also means fewer follow-up visits to your doctor.

9. It only restricts the quantity of food that you can take, but you will still be allowed to eat healthy prepared food after the operation.

10. The feeling of fullness is comfortable and normal, unlike the feeling of pain or obstruction that is associated with the adjustable band surgery.

Aside from all these advantages, more people are choosing the gastric sleeve method because it is the least expensive method among the other weight loss procedures.

4 - How do you qualify for a gastric sleeve procedure?

Adult and young adult patients who have a Body Mass Index (BMI) of 30 or more are the ideal candidates for gastric sleeve surgery. This is also recommended for obese individuals who have tried all techniques to lose weight but failed, especially the patients who are at a high risk of health problems and death.

Here are the other factors to consider in order to qualify for the procedure:

- You have a stable mental health condition.

- You have been obese for over 5 years and have tried the traditional weight loss methods but repeatedly failed.

- You are not addicted to alcohol or drugs and you don't smoke.

- For women, you must be about 100 or more pounds overweight. For men, you have to be 80 or more pounds overweight.

4 - HOW DO YOU QUALIFY FOR A GASTRIC SLEEVE PROCEDURE?

- This procedure is life-changing. You have to commit to long-term lifestyle changes in order to continue losing weight and maintain the weight that you have already lost.

5 - What are the risks and disadvantages that the procedure entails?

The complications and risks that you may suffer from after the procedure are minimal as compared to the side effects of the other weight loss surgeries. Here are the complications that you can expect following a gastric sleeve procedure:

- You will experience minor side effects immediately after the surgery. They include swelling, bleeding, bruising, and pain. For many of those who have undergone the procedure, these side effects naturally disappear several days up to a few weeks after the surgery.

- Only a few patients have complained of more severe side effects such as leaking or internal bleeding, too much pain, gastritis, and bloating in the abdominal area. There are also a small number of patients who develop pneumonia, vomiting, and infection. If you experience any of these severe side effects, make sure that you have yourself checked immediately by a doctor.

- Weight loss is gradual and may not be as great as compared to the more invasive forms of weight-loss surgeries.

- Less than 1 percent of the gastric sleeve patients experience blood clots, which can be fatal.

- It is important that you change your lifestyle after the procedure. You have to strictly follow the diet restrictions or else, the sleeve will stretch out and you will gain weight.

6 - What is the next step to do if you are interested to undergo gastric sleeve surgery?

Ask around or research for the qualified medical team that is an expert in the field and near your area. Make an appointment and consult with the doctor to learn what other things you need to prepare for before the operation.

Make sure that you know or have jotted down the following details:

- Your medical history including anesthesia complications. You will also be asked about the health history of your parents and siblings.

- Make a list of the drugs over-the-counter or prescription-type, food or herbal supplements, and vitamins that you regularly take.

- Ask your doctor about the available payment methods. If you are insured, be sure to ask what portion of the process is covered by the insurance.

- Ask all your concerns and anything that will make it

easier for you to prepare for the operation.

You have to prepare your body for the drastic changes that you will implement after the surgery. Exercise more often. You can start by walking for several minutes at the start of your day.

If you are a smoker, it is best to quit as soon as you have set your mind to undergo the procedure. Smoking makes the lungs more sensitive during the process. This makes you at a high risk of pneumonia. This will also make the healing process slow because the effects of smoking make the blood vessels narrow, which restricts your blood flow.

Due to the risks involved with smokers, many surgeons do not operate on patients who are smokers. Aside from the interview, they will require you to undergo tests to check the nicotine levels in your system before approving your request.

You must also expect drastic changes in your diet before and after the procedure. To help you cope easily with these changes, start implementing the following diet preparation tips:

1. Avoid drinking high sugar drinks until you are no longer craving for them. Avoid drinking carbonated drinks because they tend to make you feel full faster and could potentially stretch your stomach after the operation.

2. Learn how to prepare your meals in different ways aside from frying. You have to start cutting down your intake of fried food.

3. Start getting used to drinking fluids in between meals and not with meals. This is something that you will practice for a lifetime after the procedure.

4. Start using a sugar substitute instead of table sugar.

5. Start cutting down your alcohol intake. Alcohol contains empty calories that have no place in your diet after the operation.

6. You have to start chewing your food thoroughly. Decrease the portion sizes of each meal and eat three meals a day.

7. Eat healthily and focus on proteins.

8. Gather a support group. Research about online for-
   ums and groups that you can join to discuss the situation with before and after the surgery. You also need
   to talk to your friends and family about the situation.
   You need a strong support to help you in many ways,
   especially in the emotional aspect of the process.

7 - What should you expect weeks and days before you undergo the operation?

Before the operation, you've already had a number of consultations with your surgeon. You will be asked to undergo different exams and lab tests. At this point, you must already have adapted to the drinking and eating restrictions.

Two weeks prior the surgery, your surgeon will require you to follow a special diet. This will prepare your body for the procedure and increase the chance for a successful outcome. Many of those who suffer from severe obesity have enlarged livers. This condition will make the surgery difficult to perform. The diet aims to reduce the size of the liver and the amount of fat in the abdominal area.

The directives about the diet must come from your surgeon. Here's a peek at what the diet looks like to give you an idea of what you need to prepare yourself for:

- Limit your calorie intake to 1000 to 1200 each day.

- Your diet must contain low fat and low carbohydrate.

- You are required to take 6 to 8 glasses of fluids each day in order to prevent dehydration. Aside from water, you can take other sugar-free, non-carbonated, low-calorie, and caffeine-free liquids.

- Your diet must contain lots of protein. You may also be instructed to take protein supplements. This is important to protect your muscle tissues and help your body recover faster after the operation.

- You will be asked to take one protein shake for breakfast and lunch, and a lean protein and salad for dinner.

Protein supplements can be bought as powders or ready-to-drink. Here are some insightful tips for making your own protein shake:

- Add the protein supplement to plain non-fat yogurt. Mix well until combined.

- If your system cannot tolerate dairy, you can use plain soy milk or fat-free Lactaid milk.

- Pour skim milk into ice cube molders. Put into a blender once firm and process until slushy.

- Make a protein shake latte by adding a teaspoon of decaffeinated instant coffee.

Here are the other food items that are typically included in this diet 2 weeks before the procedure:

- Vegetable juice or V8

- Soup and broth without any solid particle

- Extremely thin cream of wheat or cream of rice

- Sugar-free beverages

- Protein and meal replacement shakes

At this point, you can no longer take your liquids with meals. Take them 30 minutes before and after eating. Always remember to sip them slowly.

If you want to eat solid food, get the approval of your doctor first. If he/she agrees, you can have a couple of servings of lean meat and vegetables.

What if instead of losing weight, you incur a significant increase in your weight during this period? Your doctor will adjust the date of your surgery up to the time that you have lost 10 to 15 pounds prior to the operation.

Your doctor will only allow you to take protein shakes a day before the surgery. After 5 PM, you need to consume clear liquids, such as tea, Jell-O, ginger ale, broth, and water. You cannot take anything after midnight so that your stomach will be empty by the time of the operation.

Before the surgery, ask your doctor for the kind of support that they offer throughout the recovery process. List out the hospital and your medical team's emergency contact numbers so that you would know who to turn to when something strange happens while you are recovering from home.

Arrange for someone to accompany you to the hospital. If you live alone, ask someone to stay with you at home even for several days after the procedure. Your movements will be limited for the first few days during the recovery period. The least that you want to happen is to get stressed. You will

need a lot of assistance in doing cooking and certain hy-
gienic tasks.

Make sure that you have the following items at home before
the operation:

- Canned broth

- Doctor-approved protein shakes and meal replace-
  ments

- Sugar substitutes and sugar-free flavors

- Soups with smooth texture

- No-sugar-added pudding, popsicles, and Jell-O

- Doctor-approved vitamins and minerals

- Small food containers, freezer bags, and kitchen tools

- Blender or food processor

8 - What should you expect after the operation?

Sleeve gastrectomy reduces the size of your stomach by up to 90 percent. Do not expect that you will lose weight immediately after the surgery. It is a process that requires your cooperation. There is a diet plan that is classified according to stages to help you in the healing process.

The size of your stomach a couple of hours after the surgery can hold about 2 ounces of nourishment. How will the first few hours after the operation be like?

- A nurse will monitor whatever pain you are feeling. The medication will pass through an IV and the amount of medication will depend on your initial level of pain. Prepare yourself because it can really get painful and it worsens through the hours.

- When you are already fully awake, a nurse will encourage and assist you to walk. This will help improve the functions of your urinary tract and gastrointestinal tract that slowed down after the operation. Walking will lower your risk of post-operation complications. This helps in maintaining your normal breathing function and encourages the movement of oxygen throughout your system.

- After the surgery, you will be allowed small sips of liquid or ice chips to stay hydrated. Your IV will be removed once your stomach can tolerate sufficient liquids to keep you hydrated.

- If there are no complications and the doctor sees you fit to go home, you will be allowed to do so on the second day of your hospital stay.

9 - The 5 Stages of a Gastric Sleeve Diet

You will follow a 5-stage diet plan upon coming home. In order to help your body recover faster, eat food rich in nutrients and vitamins. After you have fully recovered, your diet will be more restricted and nutritionally-balanced.

Here are the general rules on what to do in order to avoid complications and other problems after the procedure:

1. Make it a habit of eating your food and drinking fluids in a slow manner. Consume each meal for at least 30 minutes. Eating and drinking too quickly may cause nausea and vomiting.

2. Chew your food thoroughly and until it already has a liquid consistency before swallowing.

3. Do not drink fluids while eating. This is necessary to avoid the expansion of the stomach due to bloating. Drink your fluids 30 to 60 minutes before and after meals.

4. Follow the daily amount of fluids and food that your doctor recommends. It is important that you don't

gain weight during the recovery stage. If you will get bigger, this might lead to a rupture that will jeopardize the process.

5. Avoid dehydration by following the recommended amount of fluids according to the diet phase that you are in. Dehydration can lead to vomiting and diarrhea.

6. Avoid high caloric food with minimal nutrients and those with high sugar content. These foods will make it more difficult for you to lose weight.

10 - The 5 Stages of a Gastric Sleeve Diet

Clear Fluids (1 to 2 days after the operation)

This will begin upon waking up in the hospital after the operation. Your fluid intake is limited to 30 cubic centimeters of water every hour. Keep a fluid record sheet to monitor how much you have already taken.

For the first day, drink 15 ml of clear fluids every 15 minutes. Aside from water, you can also consume broth, tea, no-sugar-added Jell-O, and diluted fruit juice. You won't get dehydrated despite the restricted amount of fluid because you will still be on an IV at this point.

On your second day, you will follow the same diet in the hospital upon coming home. Slowly sip 30 ml of clear fluid every 15 minutes.

11 - Liquid Diet (Weeks 1 and 2 following the procedure)

This diet will begin on the third day after the operation. You need to drink up to 4 cups of water and take at least 70 grams of protein per day. You will also begin taking the chewable vitamins and supplements recommended by your health team.

What are you allowed to take during this phase?

Beverages

- Sugar-free clear fluids

- Water

Soups (smooth, strained, and free of lumps)

- Butternut soup

- Potato soup

- Tomato soup

Protein sources

- Skim milk or 1 percent milk

- Lactose-free milk

- Plain or natural soy drink

- Protein powder

- Protein shakes

- No sugar added yogurt

- Cottage cheese

Vegetable and Fruit

- Tomato juice

- Unsweetened apple juice

Starch and grain

- Cream of wheat

- Oatmeal (with less than 10 grams of sugar)

Keep in touch with your health team. Observe how your body responds to the new diet scheme. If you experience nausea, vomiting, and severe abdominal pain, go back to the first diet plan for the next 24 hours. If the problems continue for more than 12 hours, call your doctor and ask for an advice.

Recommended Multivitamins (liquid and chewable):

1. Multivitamin. Take 1 tablet twice a day of a chewable supplement rich in vitamins and minerals.

2. Calcium sources. Take the following chewable tablets twice each day: Caltrate 600 + D, Calcium Citrate + D, and Viactiv Calcium + D. Each tablet must contain at least 600 mg of calcium and 400 IU of vitamin D.

3. Vitamin B12 sublingual. Take a tablet each day by putting it under your tongue until it dissolves.

Always consult your nutritionist before buying any vitamins

and supplements. It is important that you those that meet your nutritional requirements depending on the diet stage that you are in.

Sample meal plan for a day:

Breakfast: Vanilla-Strawberry shake and 1 small pack of no sugar added low-fat yogurt

Snack: A cup of protein shake

Lunch: 1/4 cup of low-fat cottage cheese, 1/4 cup of plain low-fat yogurt, and 1/4 cup tomato juice

Snack: Half a cup of protein shake

Dinner: 1/4 cup of applesauce and 1/4 cup of strained cream of chicken soup with protein powder

Snack: Half a cup of protein shake

Here's a sample meal plan for those who are lactose intolerant or developed this complication after the procedure:

Breakfast: 1/4 cup of tomato juice, 1/2 cup of strained

potato soup with 1 tablespoon of protein powder, oatmeal, and peach chai protein shake.

Oatmeal is prepared by putting 1/2 cup of oats in a bowl and mixing it with 1 cup of lactose-free milk.

To prepare the peach chai protein shake, put the following ingredients in a blender: 1/3 cup of unsweetened soy beverage, 1/2 fresh peach, 1/3 cup of brewed Chai tea, 1 scoop of vanilla protein powder, 1/4 teaspoon of pumpkin pie spice, and 2 ice cubes. Process until smooth.

Lunch: 1/2 cup of strained potato soup with 1 tablespoon of unflavored protein powder.

Snack: Protein water

To make protein water, mix 1 scoop of unflavored protein powder, 1 cup of water, and 1 packet of crystal light in a container. Cover and shake well until combined.

Dinner: 1/4 cup of applesauce, 1/2 cup of strained vegetable soup with 1 tablespoon of protein powder.

Snack: 1/4 cup cream of wheat

12 - Pureed Diet (Weeks 3 and 4 after the operation)

At this stage, you will reintroduce your stomach to food that you used to eat before the operation but in soft and pureed forms. The process should be gradual. Remember to always take it easy and keenly observe how your body reacts to what you are eating. If you experience any pain or if you vomit after eating, go back to the previous diet. Let 24 hours pass before going back to this diet.

Vomiting is likely to happen at this point. Take note of the food that made you feel sick. Remove it from your menu for the next 2 to 3 weeks. You can still eat all the food items from the past diet phases though. Continue to take chewable vitamins and the mineral and protein supplements.

You must also remember to take up to 1.5 liters of calorie-free liquids each day. To make it easier to meet the daily protein requirement of 70 grams, you can add unflavored protein powder to your food and consume 2 protein shakes each day.

What are you allowed to take during this phase?

Vegetables and fruits

- Tomato juice

- Unsweetened applesauce

- Cooked or canned pureed vegetables and fruits

Starch and grains

- Cream of wheat

- Cold cereal soaked in milk

- Oatmeal with less than 10 grams of sugar

- Soda crackers

- Melba toast

All kinds of pureed soups

Beverages

- Water

- Decaffeinated tea or coffee

- Juice diluted in water

- Low-fat vegetable or meat broth

- Sugar-free clear fluids

Desserts

- No sugar added Jell-O

- No sugar added ice cream

- No sugar added pudding

Protein sources

- Protein shakes

- Skim milk or 1 percent milk

- Lactose-free milk

- Protein powder

- Ricotta cheese

- Cream cheese

- Cottage cheese

- No sugar added yogurt

- Moist and mashed fish

- Plain or natural soy beverage

- Pureed meat, including chicken, beef, and pork

- Hummus

- Soft poached egg

How to poach an egg:

Boil 2-inch deep of water in a small pan. Turn the heat to low once the water is boiling. Crack an egg into a bowl. Carefully lower the bowl into the water and let the egg slip out. Cook until done but soft.

Sample meal plan for a day:

12 - PUREED DIET (WEEKS 3 AND 4 AFTER THE OPERATION)

Breakfast: 2 tablespoons of pureed fruit, 1/3 cup of cream of wheat mixed with 4 tablespoons of milk

Snack: A cup of protein shake

Lunch: 1 soft poached egg and 2 pieces of Melba toast

Snack: 1 small pack of no sugar added yogurt

Dinner: 4 tablespoons of mashed fish or pureed meat, 2 tablespoons of pureed carrots and 2 tablespoons of mashed potato with 1 tablespoon of unflavored protein powder

Snack: A cup of protein shake

13 - Soft Diet (Weeks 5 to 9 after the procedure)

At this point, your daily protein requirement is 80 to 80 grams. Continue drinking protein shakes, unless your dietitian tells you otherwise. Continue taking your protein supplements. Start taking vitamins and mineral supplements in pill form.

In the beginning, break the pills into smaller pieces in order to avoid any discomfort. Increase your calorie-free fluid intake to 2 liters a day. It is also important that you slice your food into smaller pieces before you eat.

If you feel any discomfort, stop eating the food that caused the pain. Go back to the previous diet and try this phase again after a few days.

To keep your food moist and tender, it is best to prepare them using a slow cooker or a crackpot. Here's a list of the foods that you can reintroduce to your diet:

- Cereals with high fiber and low sugar

- Boiled or scrambled eggs, cooked with little or no fat

- All kinds of cheese, sliced into 1-inch pieces

- All soups

- Pita bread and tortilla wraps

- Well-toasted bread, thinly sliced

- Soft fruits, such as peeled mango, apple, and banana

- Diced or ground poultry or meat, cooked in chili, stew, or curry

- 1 tablespoon per serving of cashew butter, peanut butter, or almond butter

- Soft legumes cooked with sauce

Sample meal plan for a day:

Breakfast: 1/4 cup of ricotta cheese, 1/4 cup of no sugar added canned peaches (diced), and 1 tablespoon of bran flakes with a bit of cinnamon

Snack: Half a cup of protein shake

Lunch: 1/2 cup of bean soup, 1 cheese string, and 1 Melba toast

Snack: 1 small pack of no sugar added yogurt

Dinner: 2 tablespoons of well-cooked vegetables, 2 ounces of stewed chicken, and 1/4 cup of mashed potato

Snack: 1/4 whole wheat pita with ¼ cup of tuna and 2 teaspoons of light mayonnaise, 1/2 cup of protein shake

14 - Lifelong Healthy Eating

This is the start of your regular diet. This is a lifelong process and you have to stick to it in order to keep losing weight and maintain your ideal shape. You will gradually decrease the number of protein supplements that you are taking. Instead, you will consume more protein with the food that you eat. Avoid taking sweets, such as ice cream and cookies, fats, cheap calories, junk food, and high-calorie liquids.

More Tips to Make the Diet Work

1. Stop eating once your body tells you that it is full.

2. Avoid eating junk food and sweets. Eat solid food instead to relieve hunger and forget about your cravings.

3. If you feel hungry in between meals, drink instead of eating. You may only be thirsty and not hungry. You can also snack on any food items with no calories. Train yourself to eat only during meal times.

4. It is up to you to make the operation successful. You have to stick to the 5-stage diet plan during the recov-

ery period and change your diet for a lifetime. You cannot go back to your old ways before the surgery. The diet has to be teamed up with regular exercise and healthy lifestyle.

5. Pre-portion your meal by using a small plate. Always eat in a slow manner and chew your food well. Stop whenever you feel full even if you still haven't finished your meal. Refrigerate your food instead and reheat when it is time for the next meal.

6. Monitor your protein intake. If you haven't reached your daily protein goal of 60 to 80 grams when it is already night time, supplement by preparing and taking a protein shake.

15 - What are the foods rich in protein?

This list contains food that you can include in your diet to help you meet your daily protein requirement. The list includes how many grams of protein you can get per serving of each food item:

Milk and alternatives

- 1/3 cup of plain, flavored, low-fat, or regular yogurt – 4 grams

- 1/2 cup of 1 percent skim milk – 4 grams

- 1/2 cup of plain soy drink – 3 grams

- 1/3 cup of plain Greek yogurt – 8 grams

- 1/2 cup of 1 or 2 percent cottage cheese – 8 grams

- 1 slice of regular or processed cheese – 3 grams

- 2 tablespoons of skim milk powder – 5 grams

- 1-inch cube of light Mozzarella cheese – 7 grams

- 1-inch cube of regular Mozzarella cheese – 6 grams

- 1-inch cube of cheddar cheese – 7 grams

- 1/4 cup of part-skim or whole ricotta cheese – 7 grams

Chicken and meat

- 1/4 cup of chopped deli ham – 6 grams

- 1/4 cup of diced chicken – 10 grams

- 1/4 cup of diced beef steak or beef roast – 11 grams

- 1/4 cup of chopped deli turkey breast – 6 grams

- 1/4 cup of diced pork – 10 grams

- 1/4 cup of crumbled lean beef – 9 grams

- 1/4 cup of diced turkey – 10 grams

Fish

- 1/4 cup of chopped smoked salmon – 6 grams

- 1/4 cup of fresh or canned tuna – 10 grams

- 1/4 cup of shrimp – 8 grams

- 1/4 cup of canned or filet salmon – 9 grams

- 1/4 cup of scallops – 8 grams

- 1/4 cup any variety of flaked fish – 9 grams

Meat alternatives

- 1/4 cup of lentils – 5 grams

- 1/4 cup of baked canned beans – 3 grams

- 1/4 cup of kidney beans – 5 grams

- 1/4 cup of chickpeas – 4 grams

- 1/2 cup of chili – 9 grams

- 1 tablespoon of peanut butter – 4 grams

- 1/4 cup of soft tofu – 3 grams

- 1/2 cup of split pea or bean soup – 9 grams

- 1/4 cup of dry textured vegetable protein – 12 grams

- 1/4 cup of edamame – 6 grams

- 1/4 cup of hummus – 5 grams

- 1 egg white – 3 grams

- 1/4 cup of firm tofu – 5 grams

- 1 egg (whole) – 6 grams

- 1 egg yolk – 3 grams

- 1/3 cup of meatless ground meat – 10 grams

After you have achieved your weight loss goal in a span of 6 months to a year, your daily calorie requirement will increase to 1000 to 1200. Your lifelong diet will change not only with regards to what you eat but also on how you eat your food. Always remember to:

Avoid drinking fluids along with your meals. Drink 30 or 60 minutes before and after meals.

- Chew your food thoroughly and swallow only when it

has a liquefied consistency.

- Eat a small portion of food at a time and stop eating once you already feel full.

- Avoid fast food, oily, and fatty food.

- Bring a healthy snack with you wherever you go in order to avoid the temptation to eat whatever is available when hunger strikes.

- Avoid high calorie and carbonated drinks.

Follow your doctor's advice when it comes to exercise. He/she will tell you once your body can handle the activity and the kinds of exercises you can do depending on the progress of your recovery.

16 - The Emotional Pitfalls and the Most Common Complications of the Surgery

No matter how determined you are to lose weight, there will always be emotional and psychological challenges once you have undergone the surgery. These challenges will depend on how long you have been obese.

Obesity is associated with lack of self-confidence, low self-esteem, and depression. You used to deal with these emotions by eating a lot. This is a habit that you have to overcome once you have decided to undergo the procedure but it won't be easy.

Weight loss surgery is a major operation that entails a lot of drastic changes in all aspects of your life. You can help yourself by staying fit physically and mentally. Find a doctor who can counsel you and your support groups, including your family and friends. This will help a lot, especially at times when you feel like giving up.

What are the most common emotional pitfalls that you may face after the operation?

Anxiety. After the surgery, you may get overwhelmed with the new social activities and new situations that you would want to try but too scared to proceed. It is okay to feel anxious, especially in the beginning. Ask support from people who care about you to talk and push you towards trying out new things. Consult and ask a therapy if your anxiety becomes too much to handle.

Insecurity. It will take time to remove your old image from your mind and accept that you are no longer the fat person that you considered normal. There will always be a feeling of insecurity with how you look and how other people see you even after you have lost a lot of weight.

Talk to people who have experienced the same thing. Hang out with groups composed of individuals who have undergone the same procedure.

Relationship changes. If you are in a relationship, open your mind that the changes will not only affect you but also your partner. It can either make good relationships better but can also make it worse. The improved physical appearance can result in a healthy intimacy and active sex life.

On the other hand, this can also make your partner feel insecure or jealous. Before the relationship turns sour, seek counseling as a couple and go through this together. You have to reassure your partner, and both of you need to be open about your feelings towards each other.

Depression. Not everything will be pretty after the surgery. You won't lose weight immediately after coming home from the hospital. The strict diet is not easy to follow. After the surgery, you will be faced with sagging skin here and there, especially when you are beginning to lose weight. Set your expectations right. Help yourself to deal with the changes and effects of the surgery as they happen.

When things and emotions get too much to handle, always ask emotional support from your family and friends. Never hesitate to go to your doctor when the emotional turmoil won't get away. Keep yourself busy with sports, hobbies,

and other activities that will help in keeping your mind off
from the emotional and psychological setbacks of the surgery.

17 - Ways to Adjust Emotionally and Physically after the Surgery

Keep a diary or a journal. Write everything – your thoughts, struggles, the feeling of joy and accomplishments. Write everything down. Keep track of the food that you eat, the food that made you feel sick, activities that you have tried, and so on. You can always read your entries at times when you feel like giving up and turning to your old habits.

Writing about how you feel and what you are going through will help you to easily cope and adjust to the changes. This is your way to talk to yourself and understand your own emotions regarding the effects of the surgery.

Move on and adapt to the changes but do not forget what you have gone through that led you to undergo the proced-ure. It will make it easier for you to accept the new you if you will remember how it was before.

Ask for help whenever you feel like you need to. Do not keep your problems to yourself. Accept that you will need a lot of support from groups, from your loved ones, and counseling sessions with your doctor. By opening up and meeting people who have experienced the same things that you are going through, you will feel that you are not alone.

Do not be too hard on yourself. Set realistic goals and write them down in your diary. You can modify the goals depending on how your body is recovering from the operation.

Keep track of your body measurements. Take pictures of yourself to make it easier for you to monitor your physical changes. Keep your old clothes. Wearing them after you have achieved your ideal weight will give you a sense of fulfillment.

This will help you a lot, especially at times when you experience a weight loss plateau. This will serve as a visual reference to help you erase the image of your old self and remind you that you are losing weight.

Try different things. Experience and live life. Do not shy away from the new experiences and people that you meet.

Take your doctor's advice seriously. Follow his/her recommendations regarding the diet, exercises, and the supplements that you are taking. You need to take lots of rest to speed up the recovery process.

18 - The Most Common Complications of Gastric Sleeve Surgery

Most complications are likely to happen due to the changes in your digestive tract. The best that you can do to reduce your risk of having any of these is to stick to your diet and keep yourself fit. It is also important that you don't drink any alcoholic beverages for the first 6 months after the operation to avoid the risk of having an ulcer.

Dehydration

This common complication of the procedure is a signal that your body lacks fluid. The smaller size of your pouch makes it harder to drink sufficient liquid. How would you know that you are already dehydrated?

- You are constantly thirsty.

- Your urine is dark-colored and you urinate less often.

- Headache and dizziness

- Dry mouth, lips, skin, and eyes

- Feeling annoyed and tired

Make sure that you drink up to 6 cups of water each day to avoid getting dehydrated. You can also suck on ice chips and popsicles because they count as fluids, too. You can add flavors to your water to tweak its taste.

Infused ice cubes. Put an herb, a slice of fruit or a combination of these two in an ice cube tray. Pour boiling water to instantly release the flavors and aromatic compounds of the herbs. Leave to cool before freezing.

Cucumber and mint. Rinse the cucumber, thinly sliced, and put into a pitcher full of water. Add mint and put the pitcher in the fridge. The longer it stays in the fridge before you drink it, the more flavors the water will have. Add more water to reuse the flavors. Discard after 3 days and replace with new mint and cucumber slices.

Watermelon. Slice the fruit into cubes. Put them in a pitcher full of water. You can add mint if preferred. Refrigerate for a couple of hours before drinking.

Basil and blueberries. Rinse the basil and blueberries. Put the basil in a pitcher full of water. Crush the berries before mixing them with the water. Refrigerate before drinking.

Sugar-free lemonade and berries. Squeeze a couple of drops of sugar-free lemonade into a pitcher full of water. Grate the strawberries and add them to the water. Add a few slices of lemon. Refrigerate before consuming.

Hypoglycemia

The symptoms of hypoglycemia or low blood sugar include dizziness, hunger, and cold and clammy skin. These symptoms typically show up after eating foods that are high in sugar, but they naturally go away after some hours. Here are the ways to prevent this kind of complication:

- Eat balanced meals and always eat on time.

- Make sure that your meals and snacks are filled with protein.

- Take carbs that are high in fiber and low in sugar.

Have a blood glucose meter handy at home to make it easier for you to monitor your blood sugar levels. The levels must not go lower than 4 millimoles per liter, or else you must take precaution and perform the following actions:

1. Consume 15 grams of fast-acting sugar. You can take any of the following: 3 dextrose tablets, 1 tablespoon of sugar mixed with 2 tablespoons of water, 3/4 cup of juice, and 1 tablespoon of honey.

2. Lay down to rest for at least 15 minutes.

3. Check your blood sugar and repeat the first 2 steps if the result is still not higher than 4 millimoles per liter. Continue repeating the first 2 steps until the result reflects your goal.

4. Snack on items with protein and carbs, which include the following:

- Apple with peanut butter

- Hummus and carrots

- Greek yogurt with fruit slices

- Melba toast with cheese

Diarrhea

Your body is trying to adjust to the effects of the procedure. It is also trying to cope with the changes in its digestive mechanism. Diarrhea can also be a sign of a dumping syndrome. If you experience this complication, make sure that you avoid the following food:

- Milk products

- Caffeinated drinks

- Fatty food

- Food with high sugar alcohol content

Eat food items with soluble fiber, which include applesauce, oatmeal, and bananas. You can also take a dietitian-approved fiber supplement. This complication is not alarming but consult with your doctor if it lasts for more than 3 days.

Food intolerance

There are certain foods that you may find hard to digest at first, which include the following:

- Dried fruit

- Rice

- Skins of fresh fruit

- Pasta

- Fried and fatty foods

- Chicken or red meat

- Milk and milk substitutes

- Bread

- Beverages and sugary products

- Chocolate and candy

These food may likely cause pain or pressure in your stomach area. Keep track of the food that made you feel that way. Consult it with your dietitian so that he/she can find the better alternative.

Dumping Syndrome

This happens when the food that you have taken travels fast from the stomach to the small intestine. As a result, you will experience the following symptoms:

- Heart palpitation

- Explosive diarrhea

- Dizziness

- Stomach pain and cramping

- Upset stomach

- Sweating

- Nausea

- Flushing

The signs can show up an hour or two after eating, but they can also happen sooner. Make sure that you don't drink fluids with your meals. This complication is likely experienced from eating any of the following:

- Sweetened yogurt

- Frozen yogurt

- Ice cream

- Gelato

- Frozen or canned fruit in syrup

- Sorbet

- Popsicles

- Regular pudding or Jell-O

- Undiluted fruit juices

- Candied or dried fruit

- Chocolate milk

- Honey

- Sweetened or sugar-coated cereal

- Cookies

- Milkshakes

- Pastries

- Muffins

- Chocolate

- Sweetened sauces

- Regular soft drinks

- Brown or white sugar

- Deep-fried food

Lactose intolerance

It is common to develop lactose intolerance after the procedure even if you were not like this before. It happens when the body doesn't produce sufficient enzymes to break down the sugar from lactose and milk products. The signs of this complication include the following:

- Diarrhea

- Bloating and gas

- Stomach pain and cramping

Try the following steps to deal with the problem:

- Consume lactose-free milk products.

- Eat yogurt of cheese instead of drinking milk.

- Take a liquid or chewable enzyme supplement before taking or eating milk products.

19 - Gastric Sleeve Appetizer Recipes

Here are the appetizer recipes that you can try and serve starting from the phase 5 of the diet and for the rest of your life.

Bacon Wrapped Chicken with Jalapeno

Yield: 30 pieces

Ingredients:

- 1 tablespoon each of onion powder, garlic powder, and freshly ground black pepper

- 1 onion, sliced into 30 strips

- 15 jalapeno peppers, halved and seeds removed

- 1 pound chicken breasts, skinless and boneless

- 1 pound bacon, sliced

- 2 teaspoon seasoned salt

- 1 teaspoon paprika

- Blue cheese salad dressing

Directions:

1. Slice the meat into 30 pieces strips.

2. Put together the salt, pepper, paprika, onion powder, and garlic powder in a Ziploc bag. Add the meat strips, seal the bag and shake. Put 1 chicken strip and 1 onion strip in each jalapeno half. Wrap with bacon.

3. Grill until the chicken is cooked and the bacon is crisp. This will take around 20 to 30 minutes. Turn once.

4. Serve the grilled bacon wrapped chicken with jalapeno with the dressing.

Deviled Eggs with Avocado

Yield: 1 dozen

Ingredients:

- 1/4 cup olive oil mayonnaise

- 5 slices bacon (center-cut), fried and crumbled

- 1 tablespoon each red onion (finely diced) and Dijon mustard

- Sea salt and paprika to taste

- 6 eggs, hard-boiled and peeled

- Parsley sprigs

Directions:

1. Slice the eggs in half. Scoop the yolks and put them in a bowl. Add the mustard and mayonnaise to the yolks. Mix and stir in the bacon, salt, and avocado.

2. Put a tablespoon of the mixture to each half of the egg white. Sprinkle paprika on top and garnish with parsley sprig. Loosely cover with foil and chill before serving.

Spinach Artichoke Dip

Yield: 16 servings

Ingredients:

- 1 10-ounce package frozen spinach, thawed, chopped, and drained

- 5 bacon slices (center-cut), fried and crumbled

- 2 garlic cloves, minced

- 1/3 cup olive oil mayonnaise

- Cooking spray

- 1 teaspoon Herbes de Provence

- 2/3 cup Parmesan cheese, grated and divided

- 2 8-ounce packages cream cheese (with reduced-fat, room temperature

- 1 14-ounce can artichoke hearts, quartered, chopped, and drained

Directions:

1. In a bowl, put the cream cheese, mayonnaise, and garlic. Beat until mixed and creamy. Add the bacon,

spinach, half of the cheese, and artichoke hearts, and stir.

2. Transfer the mixture to a greased baking dish. Sprinkle the rest of the cheese on top. Bake in a pre-heated oven at 350 degrees for 25 minutes.

This is best served with veggies and grain crackers.

Apple and Cranberry Salsa

Yield: 4 cups

Ingredients:

- 1 jalapeno pepper, seeds removed and sliced into strips

- 1 12-ounce package cranberries (fresh or frozen), rinsed and drained

- 1/4 cup fresh cilantro leaves

- 2 apples, cored and chunked

- 1/3 cup unsweetened applesauce

- 1/2 sweet red pepper, seeds removed and chunked

- 1 teaspoon grated lime peel

- 1/2 red onion, chunked

- 1 lime, juiced

- Sea salt and freshly ground black pepper to taste

- 1/2 cup sugar substitute

Directions:

1. Put all the ingredients in a blender. Pulse until chopped.

2. Transfer to a bowl, cover and refrigerate for an hour before serving.

Crispy Cheese

Yield: 8 crisps

Ingredients:

- 1/2 cup hard cheese, grated

Directions:

1. Put a tablespoonful of cheese on a baking sheet lined with parchment paper. Press it into a thin circle. Repeat the process until you have used all the cheese. Leave a distance of about 2 inches in between the circles.

2. Bake in a preheated oven at 350 degrees for 15 minutes. Allow to cool before serving.

Spicy Pinto Bean Sauce

Yield: 2 cups

Ingredients:

- 1 teaspoon cumin

- 1 30-ounce can pinto beans, rinsed and drained

- 1/4 teaspoon each of sea salt, ground black pepper, and red pepper flakes

- 1/2 cup each of cream cheese (with reduced fat), water, and light sour cream

- 2 garlic cloves, minced

- 1 cup Mexican cheese blend, divided

- 1/2 teaspoon chili powder

Directions:

1. Put water, garlic, and beans in a food processor with a metal blade attachment. Pulse until almost mashed.

2. Transfer the mixture to a pan over medium heat. Season with salt, pepper, chili powder, cumin, and red pepper flakes. Stir in half a cup of cheese, sour cream, and cream cheese. Mix until combined.

3. Remove from heat once the mixture is heated through. Transfer to a heat-proof bowl. Sprinkle the rest of the cheese on top. Microwave for 40 seconds on a high setting.

This is best served with veggies and chips.

Shrimp with Cocktail Dipping

Yield: 10-12

Ingredients:

- 1/3 cup chili sauce

- 2 tablespoons prepared horseradish

- 2 teaspoons Old Bay seasoning

- 1 tablespoon fresh lemon juice

- 2/3 cup ketchup

- Chopped celery

- 1 teaspoon Worcestershire sauce

- 1/2 teaspoon lemon zest

- 2 pounds shrimp, peeled, deveined and cooked

Directions:

1. Put the cooked shrimp on a plate and lightly sprinkle with the seasoning.

2. In a bowl, mix the rest of the ingredients, except for the celery. Garnish the dipping with chopped celery

and serve along with the shrimp.

Healthy White Bean Hummus

Yield: 1 1/2 cups

Ingredients:

- 2 garlic cloves, minced

- 1/4 cup each of water and extra-virgin olive oil

- 1/2 teaspoon sea salt

- 1 lemon, juiced

- 1/3 cup tahini

- 1 15-ounce can white beans, rinsed and drained

Directions:

1. Put all the ingredients in a food processor with a metal blade attachment. Process until smooth.

2. Transfer to a bowl. Serve along with veggies or pita chips.

You can opt to top the hummus with chopped artichoke hearts or roasted bell peppers.

Mushroom Pizza

Yield: 12 mushrooms

Ingredients:

- 1/4 cup each of turkey pepperoni slices and grated Parmesan cheese

- 12 whole Crimini mushrooms

- Cooking spray

- 2 tablespoons each of sliced black olives and Italian-leaf parsley

- Garlic salt and ground black pepper to taste

- 1/8 of red onion, sliced

- 1/4 of green bell pepper, sliced

- 1/2 cup cream cheese (with reduced-fat), room temperature

- 1/2 teaspoon Italian seasoning

Directions:

1. Remove the stems of the mushrooms and wash with a damp cloth.

2. Put the rest of the ingredients in a food processor with a metal blade attachment. Process until combined with small chunks.

3. Put a spoonful of the mixture on each mushroom cap.

4. Arrange the stuffed mushrooms on a greased baking sheet. Bake in a preheated oven at 350 degrees for 20 minutes. Set the oven to broil and brown the tops of the mushrooms.

Thai Chicken Satay

Yield: 4-6 servings

Ingredients:

- 1 pound chicken tenders

- 1 lime, juiced

- 1 tablespoon each of fish sauce and soy sauce (low-sodium)

- 1/2 teaspoon chili garlic sauce

- 2 tablespoons sesame oil

For the peanut sauce

- 2 tablespoons peanut butter (smooth natural)

- 1 teaspoon brown sugar

- 1 tablespoon each of soy sauce (low-sodium), sesame oil, and fresh lime juice

- 2 tablespoons of light coconut milk

- 1/2 teaspoon chili garlic sauce

Directions:

1. In a shallow dish, combine the soy sauce, sesame oil, chili garlic sauce, fish sauce, and lime juice. Marinate the meat for 15 minutes.

2. Put 2 marinated chicken tenders on each skewer. Wrap the end of the skewer with foil. Grill both sides of the meat until cooked.

3. Prepare the sauce by whisking the chili garlic sauce, peanut butter, lime juice, coconut milk, brown sugar, soy sauce, and sesame oil in a bowl.

4. Serve the grilled along with the sauce.

Stuffed Bell Peppers

Yield: up to 40 stuffed baby peppers

Ingredients:

- 20 baby bell peppers

- 2 garlic cloves, minced

- 1 teaspoon ground cumin

- 1/2 teaspoon sea salt

- 1/2 14.5-ounce can diced tomatoes (juice included)

- 1/2 15-ounce can black beans, rinsed and drained

- 1 4-ounce can mild diced green chilies (juice included)

- 1 tablespoon chili powder

- 1 1/2 cups Mexican cheese, shredded and divided

- 1/2 cup onion, chopped

- Fresh cilantro, chopped

- 1/2 pound ground turkey (99 percent fat-free)

Directions:

1. Cut each pepper in half and remove the top part, seeds, and membranes.

2. Cook turkey in a pan over medium-high flame until browned. Add garlic and onions, and cook for 4 minutes. Stir in the black beans, cumin, chilies, salt, tomatoes, and chili powder. Bring to a boil. Turn the heat to low. Simmer for 15 minutes before turning off the stove.

3. Allow the dish to slightly cool before adding a cup of

cheese and the cooked quinoa. Mix well.

4. Fill each pepper with a tablespoon of the mixture. Arrange the stuffed peppers on a baking tray and cover with foil. Bake in a preheated oven at 375 degrees for 30 minutes. Discard the foil. Sprinkle the rest of the cheese on top and bake for 5 more minutes.

5. Put chopped cilantro on top before serving.

Easy-to-Do 9-Layer Dip

Yield: 10-12 servings

Ingredients:

- 1 cup light sour cream

- 1 1.5-ounce pack taco seasoning

- 1 15-ounce can black beans, rinsed and drained

- 1 lime, juiced

- 1 cup grape tomatoes, halved

- 1 cup bottled mild salsa

- 2 tablespoons green onion, chopped

- 1 avocado, diced

- 1/2 cup fresh cilantro, chopped

- 1 1/2 cups grated cheddar cheese

- 1/2 cup red bell pepper, diced

Directions:

1. Transfer the beans to a plate. Mash them using a fork. Spread the mashed beans all over the plate. Sprinkle with the taco seasoning. Put sour cream on top of the beans. Gently spread but make sure that you do not mix salsa with the sour cream. Sprinkle cheese all over. Put the tomato halves on top. Pour lime juice all over the avocado before arranging them on top of the stack. Sprinkle the following in this order: green onions, red peppers, and cilantro.

2. Put in the fridge before serving.

Feta and Tomato Cheese Dip

Yield: 1 1/2 cups

Ingredients:

- 2 tablespoons pine nuts, toasted

- 2 tablespoons fresh basil, chopped

- 4 ounces sun-dried tomatoes (packed in oil), julienned

- 1/4 cup olive oil

- 4 garlic cloves, minced

- 4 ounces feta cheese, crumbled

Directions:

1. Put all the ingredients in a bowl. Toss to combine.

2. Serve the dip along with soft flatbread, sliced veggies, or pita chips.

Chicken Meatballs Southwestern Style

Yield: 24 small meatballs

Ingredients:

- 2 garlic cloves

- 3 green onions, trimmed

- 1 egg

- 1 1/2 pounds lean ground chicken

- 1 teaspoon cumin

- 1 jalapeño, seeds removed

- 1/4 cup fresh cilantro, chopped

- 1/2 red bell pepper, chunked

- A pinch oregano

- 1/4 cup breadcrumbs

- 1/4 teaspoon freshly ground black pepper

- 1/2 teaspoon sea salt

- Greek yogurt dressing

Directions:

1. Put the green onions, garlic, red bell pepper, cilantro, and jalapeño in a food processor with a metal blade attachment. Cover and pulse until minced.

2. Transfer the mixture to a bowl. Add the bread crumbs, ground chicken, salt, pepper, cumin, oregano, and egg. Mix thoroughly using your hands. Roll into small balls. Arrange the balls on a baking sheet lined with parchment paper. Bake in a pre-heated oven at 400 degrees for 15 minutes.

3. Serve the meatballs along with mashed avocado or Greek yogurt dressing.

20 - Gastric Sleeve Diet Breakfast Recipes

Spicy Egg Puff

Yield: 12 servings

Ingredients:

- 10 eggs

- 1/2 teaspoon salt

- 2 cups low-fat cottage cheese (2 percent)

- 4 cups Monterey Jack cheese, shredded

- 1/2 cup all-purpose flour

- 1 4-ounce can green chilies, chopped

- 1 teaspoon baking powder

Directions:

1. Beat the eggs in a bowl until fluffy.

2. In another bowl, mix the flour, salt, and baking

powder. Gradually add this to the beaten eggs. Mix until combined. Fold in the chilies and cheese.

3. Transfer the mixture to a greased baking dish. Bake in a preheated oven at 350 degrees for 40 minutes. Leave for 5 minutes before serving.

Banana-Strawberry Smoothie

Yield: 2 servings

Ingredients:

- 1/2 frozen banana

- 10 frozen strawberries

- 1/2 cup Greek yogurt (plain)

- 1 cup low-fat milk (1 percent) or light soy

- 1/2 tablespoon agave nectar

- 1 tablespoon ground flax meal

- 1 scoop whey protein powder (vanilla-flavored)

Directions:

1. Put all the ingredients in a blender. Process until smooth. Pour over 2 glasses and serve.

Cheesecake Parfait with Berries

Yield: 8

Ingredients:

- 4 ounces light cream cheese, softened

- 2 cups low-fat milk

- 1 cup sliced strawberries

- 1 cup fresh blueberries

- 1/4 teaspoon vanilla extract

- 2 tablespoons agave nectar

- 1/2 cup honey roasted almonds, chopped

- 1 4-serving package cheesecake instant pudding mix (sugar-free)

- 1 6-ounce pack strawberry cheesecake light yogurt

Directions:

1. Put the berries and agave nectar in a bowl. Mash some of the blueberries to get a little amount of juice out. Leave for 5 minutes but stir the mixture twice.

2. In another bowl, put the pudding mix, cream cheese, vanilla, yogurt, and milk. Beat for 3 minutes using an electric mixer set on medium-high speed. Cover the bowl and put in the fridge for 20 minutes.

3. Line up 8 parfait glasses. Put 2 tablespoons of the blueberry mixture in each glass. Add a tablespoonful of the cream cheese mixture and top with a table-spoon of chopped almonds. Serve immediately.

You can also cover the other glasses and put in the fridge for 8 hours before serving.

Spinach and Smoked Turkey Quiche

Yield: 12 servings

Ingredients:

- 1 cup fresh baby spinach leaves

- 1/8 tsp freshly ground black pepper

- 3/4 cup smoked turkey, cubed

- 1/2 cup fat-free half and half

- 1 teaspoon baking powder

- 3/4 cup shredded Swiss cheese, divided

- 1/2 cup chopped onion

- Cooking spray

- 2 eggs, plus 2 egg whites

- 1 cup low-fat cottage cheese (2 percent)

- 1/2 cup whole wheat pastry flour

- 1/4 cup shredded reduced-fat cheddar cheese

Directions:

1. Grease a nonstick skillet with cooking spray and place

over medium-high heat. Put the meat, pepper, and onion. Saute for 4 minutes.

2. Spread 1/4 cup of shredded Swiss cheese on a greased pie plate. Arrange the turkey mixture on top.

3. In a bowl, mix the rest of the Swiss cheese, cottage cheese, eggs and egg whites, half and half, and cheddar cheese. Whisk until combined.

4. Combine flour and baking powder in a bowl. Gradually add this to the egg mixture. Mix well. Pour this over the turkey mixture. Bake in a preheated oven at 350 degrees for 45 minutes.

Green Smoothie

Yield: 2 servings

Ingredients:

- 1 cup frozen peach chunks

- 1 cup frozen mango chunks

- 2 cups water

- 1 cup frozen pineapple chunks

- 2 tablespoons sugar substitute

- 2 cups fresh spinach, tightly packed

- 1/2 lemon, juiced

Directions:

1. Put water and spinach in a blender. Process for 2 minutes or until smooth. Add the peaches, mango, lemon juice, pineapple, and agave nectar. Process until smooth. Serve immediately.

Easy Breakfast Delight

Yield: 1 serving

Ingredients:

- 1 teaspoon chia seeds

- 1/2 apple, diced

- 1/4 cup almond milk or light vanilla soy

- 1 6-ounce pack Greek yogurt

- 1 tablespoon each of all or any of the following: toasted sunflower seeds, unsweetened shredded coconut, mini dark chocolate chips, toasted pistachio seeds, and toasted pumpkin seeds

Directions:

1. Transfer the yogurt to a bowl. Pour soy milk and top with all the ingredients. You can also use other toppings, such as chopped cashews, chopped walnuts, and toasted sliced almonds.

Crustless Vegetable Quiche

Yield: 8 servings

Ingredients:

- 3/4 cup asparagus spears, sliced

- Cooking spray

- 2 tablespoons green onion, sliced

- 1/2 green or red bell pepper, diced

- 1 tablespoon olive oil

- 2 garlic cloves, minced

- 2 cups fresh spinach leaves, packed

- 1 teaspoon ground thyme

- 1/4 cup cooked bacon, crumbled

- 4 ounces mushrooms, sliced

- 3 eggs, plus 3 egg whites

- 1/4 teaspoon freshly ground black pepper

- 1/2 teaspoon sea salt

- 1/4 cup Parmesan cheese, shredded

- 1/2 cup artichoke hearts (packed in water), chopped

- 1 1/4 cup cheddar cheese, shredded

- 3/4 cup fat-free half and half

Directions:

1. Heat oil in a pan over medium-high flame. Stir in the asparagus, artichoke hearts, garlic, green onion, thyme, mushrooms, spinach, and bell pepper. Saute for 5 minutes. Add the crumbled bacon and season with salt and pepper. Leave to cool.

2. In a bowl, whisk the milk, salt, pepper, eggs, and egg whites.

3. Transfer the cooked vegetables to a greased pie pan. Sprinkle with shredded cheese. Pour the egg mixture and spread the shredded Parmesan cheese on top.

4. Bake in a preheated oven at 350 degrees for 45 minutes. Leave to cool for 10 minutes before slicing.

Cheesy Vegetarian Frittata

Yield: 6 servings

Ingredients:

- 1/2 zucchini, seeded and diced

- 1 tablespoon olive oil

- 2 ounces low-fat Mozzarella cheese, shredded

- 1/2 teaspoon dried ground oregano

- 4 ounces mushrooms, sliced

- 6 eggs, beaten

- 1/2 red or green, diced

- 2 ounces Parmesan cheese, shaved

- 2 ounces Feta cheese, crumbled

- 1 teaspoon seasoned salt

- 1/4 red onion, sliced

Directions:

1. Heat oil in an omelet pan over medium-high heat. Put the bell pepper, mushrooms, onion, and zucchini. Saute for 6 minutes. Turn the heat to low and add all the cheese. Leave the dish until the cheese melts. Put the eggs, oregano and seasoned salt. Cover the pan

and cook for 12 minutes.

2. Remove the cover of the pan and put it in a preheated broiler. Broil for a couple of minutes or until the top part has browned.

3. Allow to cool a bit before slicing. Serve while warm.

Ricotta and Spinach Pie

Yield: 12 muffins or 1 whole pie

Ingredients:

- 1 garlic clove, minced

- 1/8 teaspoon ground nutmeg

- 1 tablespoon olive oil

- Salt and pepper to taste

- 1/2 cup onion, chopped

- 2 cups part-skim milk ricotta cheese

- 8 cups fresh spinach, chopped

- 1/4 cup Parmesan cheese, shredded

- 1 cup mozzarella cheese, shredded

- 1 pound turkey sausage (Italian-seasoned)

- 3/4 cup egg substitute

Directions:

1. Heat oil in a pan over medium-high flame. Cook the garlic and onions for 3 minutes. Stir in the spinach and cook for 5 minutes. Put the nutmeg, mix, and season with salt and pepper. Turn off the heat and leave to cool.

2. In a bowl, combine the egg substitute, parmesan, mozzarella, and ricotta cheese, and the sautéed spinach. Roll out the sausage on top and pour the filling. Bake in a preheated oven at 350 degrees for 30 minutes.

Banana-Apple Protein Smoothie

Yield: 2

Ingredients:

- 1/2 cup apple juice (unsweetened)

- 1 banana

- 1 tablespoon ground flax meal

- 1 tablespoon almond butter

- 2 teaspoon agave nectar

- 1/2 cup light Greek yogurt (vanilla)

Directions:

1. Put all the ingredients in a blender. Add 3 ice cubes. Process until smooth. Transfer to 2 glasses and serve.

21 - Gastric Sleeve Diet Salad Recipes

Broccoli and Chicken Salad

Yield: 8 servings

Ingredients:

- 1/2 cup red onion, diced

- 2 cups cooked chicken breasts, diced

- 1/2 cup carrot, shredded

- 3 cups broccoli florets, chopped

- 1/2 cup red grapes, halved

- 8 slices of bacon (center-cut), cooked and crumbled

- 1/2 cup cashews, toasted

For the dressing:

- 1/2 cup Greek yogurt (plain non-fat)

- 1/4 teaspoon sea salt

- 1/4 cup white wine vinegar

- 1/2 cup olive oil mayonnaise

- 2 teaspoons of sugar substitute

Directions:

1. Put the broccoli in a heat-proof bowl. Microwave for 3 minutes on a high setting. Immediately rinse under cold water and drain.

2. Put the broccoli in a bowl. Add the toasted cashews, carrot, onion, grapes, chicken, and bacon. Carefully mix to combine.

3. Mix the dressing in a bowl. Combine the vinegar, mayonnaise, sugar, salt, and Greek yogurt. Mix until creamy. Pour over the salad and toss to coat. Refrigerate before serving.

White and Black Bean Greek Salad

Yield: 6 servings

Ingredients:

- 1/3 cup red onion, chopped

- 4 ounces feta cheese (reduced-fat), crumbled

- 1/3 cup fresh mint leaves, chopped

- 1 15-ounce can white beans (reduced-sodium), drained and rinsed

- 1 15-ounce can black beans (reduced-sodium), drained and rinsed

- 1/2 cup cucumber, diced

For the dressing:

- 2 tablespoons agave nectar

- 3 tablespoons fresh lemon juice

- 1/2 teaspoon each of oregano leaves, celery seed, garlic powder, sea salt, and fresh ground black pepper

- 1/4 cup olive oil

Directions:

1. In a bowl, mix the cucumber, mint, beans, red onion, and feta.

2. Whip up all the ingredients for the dressing in another bowl. Pour over the salad and toss to coat.

3. Cover the bowl and chill for an hour before serving.

Chicken Caesar Salad

Yield: 6 servings

Ingredients:

- 1 cup canned garbanzo beans (reduced-sodium), drained and rinsed

- 2 cups romaine lettuce leaves, torn

- 1/2 cup cucumber, peeled and sliced

- 2 tablespoons green onions, sliced

- 1/2 pound chicken breasts (skinless and boneless), cooked and diced

- 2 ounces shaved Parmesan cheese and crumbled sun-dried tomato

- 1 cup cherry tomatoes, halved

- 1/2 cup light Caesar dressing

- 2 tablespoons fresh basil, chopped

Directions:

1. In a bowl, mix the garbanzo beans, lettuce, tomatoes, chicken, basil, green onions, and cucumber. Add the dressing and toss to combine. Top with cheese before serving.

Grape, Melon and Chicken Salad

Yield: 6 servings

Ingredients:

- 1/2 ripe cantaloupe, peeled and sliced into bite-size pieces

- 1/4 cup each of plain Greek yogurt, chopped cashews, and reduced-fat mayonnaise

- 1/2 cup each of halved red grapes and sliced celery

- 1/2 teaspoon salt

- 1/4 teaspoon fresh ground black pepper

- 1 orange, juiced

- 2 cups cooked chicken, cubed

Directions:

1. In a bowl, mix the celery, grapes, and chicken.

2. In another bowl, combine the orange juice, mayonnaise, salt, and yogurt. Pour this over the chicken mixture and toss to combine. Top with chopped cashews before serving.

Curry Chicken Salad with Coconut

Yield: 4

Ingredients:

- 1/4 cup shredded carrots

- 1/2 cup light coconut milk

- 2 tablespoons green onions, thinly sliced

- 2 tablespoons roasted peanuts, chopped

- 2 tablespoons fresh cilantro, chopped

- 4 green leaf lettuce leaves

- 1 tablespoon Thai green curry paste

- 1/4 cup unsweetened shredded coconut

- 1/2 cup red grapes, halved

- 1 1/4 cup chicken, cooked and shredded

Directions:

1. Put the curry paste and coconut milk in a bowl. Mix until smooth. Add the green onions, carrots, peanuts, chicken, coconut, grapes, and cilantro. Toss to combine.

2. Lay a lettuce leaf on a plate. Put 1/4 of the mixture. Roll the leaf and fold the ends.

You can serve this along with fresh fruit.

Spinach Salad with Chicken and Curry Dressing

Yield: 4-6 servings

Ingredients:

- 4 cups spinach leaves, sliced

- 1/4 cup almonds, sliced

- 1/4 cup green onion, sliced

- 2 teaspoons sugar substitute

- 1/2 cup diced celery

- 1 cup diced apple

- 1 cup cooked chicken, diced

For the creamy curry dressing:

- 1/4 cup Greek lemon yogurt

- 1/4 cup light olive oil mayonnaise

- 2 tablespoons water

- 3 tablespoons fresh lemon juice

- 1 teaspoon curry powder

- Sea salt and fresh ground black pepper to taste

- 1 teaspoon sugar substitute

Directions:

1. In a skillet over medium-high flame, combine the sugar substitute and almonds. Stir for 3 minutes. Transfer the cooked almonds to a waxed paper and arrange in a single layer. Allow to cool.

2. In a bowl, mix the chicken, spinach, green onion, celery, and apple.

3. Mix all the ingredients for the dressing. Toss with the apple and vegetable mixture. Top with sweetened almonds and serve.

Chicken Caprese Salad

Yield: 8 servings

Ingredients:

- 1 pound chicken breasts (skinless and boneless)

- 5 cups Romaine lettuce leaves, rinsed and torn

- 1 tablespoon olive oil

- 1 14-ounce can artichoke hearts, drained and quartered

- 2 cups cherry tomatoes, halved

- Sea salt and freshly ground pepper to taste

- 1 avocado, sliced

- 1/4 cup basil leaves, thinly sliced

- 1 cup mini mozzarella cheese balls, halved

For the dressing:

- 1 teaspoon sugar substitute

- 1/4 cup olive oil

- 1/4 cup balsamic vinegar

- 1 teaspoon sea salt

- 1 teaspoon minced garlic

- 1 teaspoon dried basil

Directions:

1. Put all the ingredients for the dressing in a bowl. Whisk to combine. Put 4 tablespoons of the mixture in a Ziploc bag. Add the chicken. Seal the bag and leave for 30 minutes.

2. Heat a tablespoon of oil in a pan over medium-high flame. Drain the marinade and put the chicken in the pan. Cook each side for 7 minutes. Turn off the heat and leave to rest for 10 minutes. Cut the meat into strips.

3. Arrange the lettuce on a platter. Add the tomatoes,

artichoke hearts, avocado slices, chicken, and mozzarella cheese. Put the basil strips on top. Drizzle with the rest of the dressing. You can opt to season the salad with salt and pepper.

Chicken Asian Salad

Yield: 8 servings

Ingredients:

- 4 chicken breasts, boneless, skinless and halved

- 2 teaspoons Chinese Five Spice powder

- 2 tablespoons sesame oil

- 2 tablespoons reduced-sodium soy sauce

- 1/2 teaspoon garlic powder

- 1 teaspoon sugar substitute

For the salad:

- 4 cups chopped cabbage

- 1/4 cup diced red onion

- 1/4 cup chopped peanuts

- 1/4 cup chopped fresh mint leaves

- 1/4 cup chopped fresh cilantro

- 1/2 cup diced red bell pepper

- 1/2 cup cucumber, diced, peeled, and seeded

- 1/2 cup shredded carrots

For the chili lime dressing:

- 2 tablespoons lime juice

- 2 tablespoons canola oil

- 1 tablespoon agave nectar

- 1 tablespoon chili garlic sauce

- Sea salt and freshly ground black pepper to taste

- 1/4 cup seasoned rice vinegar

Directions:

1. Put the following in a Ziploc bag: Five Spice powder, sugar substitute, soy sauce, garlic powder, and oil. Add the chicken and seal the bag. Leave for an hour to marinate.

2. Put the marinated chicken on a preheated grill over medium-high flame. Grill each side for 8 minutes. Allow to cool before cutting into thin slices.

3. Mix all the salad ingredients in a bowl and put the chicken on top.

4. Put all the ingredients for the dressing in a jar. Cover the jar and shake to mix thoroughly. Pour the dressing over the salad. Sprinkle with peanuts on top before serving.

Tuna Salad

Yield: 8 servings

Ingredients:

- 4 ounces green beans, cut in half

- 3 hard-boiled eggs, peeled and sliced

- 6 small new red potatoes, scrubbed and quartered

- 1 12-ounce can albacore tuna (water-packed), drained

- 2 ripe tomatoes, cored and sliced into 8 pieces

- 1/4 cup black olives, sliced

- 1/4 red onion, thinly sliced

- 1 medium head butter lettuce, rinsed, dried, and torn

For the vinaigrette:

- 2 garlic cloves, chopped

- 1 lemon, juiced

- 1 teaspoon agave nectar

- 1/4 cup red wine vinegar

- 1/2 cup olive oil

- 1/2 teaspoon sea salt

- 1 tablespoon Dijon mustard

- 1 teaspoon Herbes de Provence

Directions:

1. Boil salted water in a large pot. Cook the red potatoes for 8 minutes. Drain water. Pour a bit of olive oil over the potatoes and toss.

2. Lay the lettuce leaves on a platter. Add the eggs, tuna, red onion, tomatoes, steamed green beans, cooked potatoes, and olives.

3. Put all the ingredients for the vinaigrette in a food processor, except for the olive oil. Process until mixed. Gradually add the oil and continue mixing until everything is combined.

4. Serve the salad along with the vinaigrette.

Steak Salad with Avocado and Blue Cheese

Yield: 6 servings

Ingredients:

- 1/4 cup sliced green onions

- 4 cups mixed salad greens

- 4 ounces blue cheese, crumbled

- 1 medium avocado, diced

- 1/2 cup fresh blueberries, rinsed

- 1 pound lean steak, grilled and sliced into strips

- 1/2 cup Greek yogurt blue cheese dressing

Directions:

1. Arrange the salad greens on a platter. Add the green onion, blueberries, crumbled blue cheese, avocado, and steak slices. Pour the dressing on top of the salad. Serve immediately.

Grilled Shrimp Salad with Greek Vinaigrette

Yield: 6 servings

Ingredients:

- 3 cups whole fresh baby spinach leaves

- 2 tomatoes, thinly sliced into wedges

- 2 garlic cloves, minced

- 1 pound fresh shrimp, peeled and deveined

- 1/4 teaspoon sea salt

- 1/2 teaspoon lemon zest

- 1/3 cup Kalamata olives

- 3 cups romaine lettuce, torn

- 1/4 cup red onion, chopped

- 1 cucumber, peeled and sliced

- 1 tablespoon butter, melted

- 1/4 cup reduced-fat feta cheese

For the Greek vinaigrette:

- 1 tablespoon each of chopped fresh oregano, red wine vinegar, agave nectar, chopped fresh mint, and lemon juice

- 1/4 teaspoon freshly ground black pepper

- 1/2 teaspoon sea salt

- 3 tablespoons olive oil

Directions:

1. Wash the shrimp and pat to dry. Put them in a bowl. Add salt, butter, garlic, and lemon zest. Toss to coat. Cover the bowl and leave for 30 minutes.

2. In another bowl, mix the romaine lettuce, spinach, red onion, olives, cucumber, and tomatoes. Set aside.

3. Insert shrimp onto 4 skewers. Put them on a pre-

heated grill and cook each side for 8 minutes.

4. Put all the ingredients for the vinaigrette in a food processor. Process until combined. Pour this over the salad. Top with grilled shrimp and feta cheese.

Grilled Salmon and Avocado-Strawberry Salad

Yield: 6 servings

Ingredients:

- 4 wild Atlantic salmon fillets

- 1 avocado, cubed

- 6 cups of fresh spring lettuce mix

- 1/4 red onion, thinly sliced

- 4 ounces feta cheese, crumbled

- 1-pint strawberries, sliced

- 1/4 cup sliced almonds, toasted

For the honey glaze:

- 1/4 teaspoon sea salt

- 1 tablespoon each of lemon juice and honey

- 1 teaspoon liquid smoke

- 2 tablespoons olive oil

For the honey balsamic dressing:

- 1 tablespoon honey

- 1/4 cup olive oil

- 1/4 teaspoon garlic powder

- 2 tablespoons balsamic vinegar

- Sea salt and freshly ground black pepper to taste

- 1 teaspoon Dijon mustard

Directions:

1. Combine all the ingredients for the honey glaze in a

small jar. Cover and shake until well-combined.

2. Rinse the salmon fillets and pat to dry. Coat them with a bit of olive oil. Put them on a preheated grill and cook each side for 5 minutes. Transfer them to a platter and brush with the honey. Set aside.

3. Arrange the spring mix into 4 plates. Top each plate with red onion, strawberries, sliced almonds, avocado, and cheese. Add more dressing and glaze.

Napoli Salad

Yield: 6 servings

Ingredients:

- 1 tomato, diced

- 3 chicken breasts (boneless and skinless)

- 1 red bell pepper, cored and sliced

- 1/4 cup red onion, sliced

- 6 cups fresh baby spinach leaves, rinsed and stems

removed

- 1/2 cup feta cheese, crumbled

- 1/3 cup bacon, cooked and crumbled

- 1 14-ounce can artichoke hearts, drained and sliced

For the balsamic vinaigrette:

- 2 garlic cloves, minced

- 1/4 cup balsamic vinegar

- 1/2 teaspoon sea salt

- 1 tablespoon Dijon mustard

- 1/2 cup olive oil

- 1/2 teaspoon dried oregano leaves

Directions:

1. Put the meat in between layers of plastic wrap. Flatten the meat by pounding using a mallet. Transfer the chicken to a bowl. Season with salt and pepper.

2. Cook each side of the seasoned chicken on a pre-heated grill for 5 minutes. Let stand for 5 minutes before cutting 8 slices per chicken breast.

3. Place the spinach leaves on a platter. Add tomatoes, red onion, chicken slices, crumbled bacon, artichoke hearts, feta cheese, and bell pepper.

4. Put the mustard, vinegar, salt, oregano, and garlic in a bowl. Whisk until mixed. Gradually add olive oil while whisking. Pour the vinaigrette over the salad. Toss the ingredients until combined.

Bean Salad with Grilled Flank Steak

Yield: 6 servings

Ingredients:

- 1/2 teaspoon steak seasoning

- 3 tablespoons reduced-sodium soy sauce

- Cooking spray

- 1/4 red onion, thinly sliced

- 1 pound flank steak, trimmed

- 1 15-ounce can black beans, drained and rinsed

- 1 15-ounce can white beans, drained and rinsed

- 1/2 cup roasted red bell peppers, chopped

- 1 tablespoon Worcestershire sauce

- 2 cups fresh green beans, sliced

For the balsamic dressing:

- 2 tablespoons extra virgin olive oil

- 1/4 teaspoon dried oregano

- 3 tablespoons balsamic vinegar

- 1/4 cup reduced-fat Feta cheese, crumbled

- Sea salt and freshly ground black pepper to taste

Directions:

1. Mix the Worcestershire sauce, pepper, and salt in a

bowl. Generously rub all sides of the meat with the mixture. Place the seasoned meat inside a Ziploc bag, seal and refrigerate for 30 minutes.

2. Cook each side of the steak on a preheated grill for 8 minutes. Once done, transfer the meat to a chopping board and cover with loose foil. Leave for 10 minutes before cutting into thin slices.

3. Steam the green beans until crisp. Soak in a bowl filled with cold water to stop from cooking. Drain and pat dry.

4. Put the green beans in a bowl. Add the black beans, white beans, red onion, red pepper, and flank steak. Gently mix to combine.

5. In another bowl, mix the vinegar and the rest of the ingredients, except for the feta cheese. Mix well. Pour the mixture over the salad. Toss to combine. Sprinkle feta cheese on top. Cover the bowl and chill before serving.

Cobb Salad Southwestern Style

Yield: 10 servings

Ingredients:

- 1 pound chicken, cooked seasoned with taco seasoning

- 1/2 red bell pepper, seeded and diced

- 1 bag mixed salad greens

- 4 slices bacon, cooked and crumbled

- 1 15-ounce can low-sodium black beans, drained and rinsed

- 1 small avocado, diced

- 1 cup Mexican style cheese, shredded

- 1/2 cup cilantro lime ranch dressing

- 1 cup grape tomatoes, halved

For the cilantro lime ranch dressing

- 2 tomatillos, husked and quartered

- 1 cup buttermilk

- 1/4 bunch fresh cilantro

- 1 cup light mayonnaise

- 1/2 fresh lime, juiced

- 1 garlic clove

- 1 pack of Ranch Buttermilk Recipe dressing mix

- 1 jalapeno pepper, seeded and halved

Directions:

1. Put the salad greens on a platter. Put the rest of the ingredients, except for the dressing, on top.

2. Put all the ingredients for the dressing in a food processor. Process until blended. Pour this over the salad. Toss to combine.

Mediterranean Tuna Salad

Yield: 6 servings

Ingredients:

- 1/3 cup Greek olives, sliced

- 2 6-ounce cans albacore tuna, drained

- 1/2 red onion, finely sliced

- 1/2 14-ounce can artichoke hearts, drained and quartered

- 2 tablespoons flat-leaf parsley, chopped

- 1 tablespoon fresh oregano, chopped

- 2 garlic cloves, minced

- 1/4 cup red bell pepper, chopped

- Salt and freshly ground pepper to taste

- 2 tablespoons chopped fresh basil

- 2 tablespoons lemon juice

- 1/4 cup light mayonnaise

Directions:

1. Put all the ingredients in a bowl. Toss to combine.

Asian Salad with Grilled Shrimp

Yield: 6 servings

Ingredients:

- 3/4 cup Thai Peanut Dressing, divided

- 1 pound large fresh shrimp, peeled and deveined

- 2 tablespoons each of fresh lime juice, creamy peanut butter, and unseasoned rice vinegar

- 1 tablespoon each of chopped fresh mint leaves, reduced-sodium soy sauce, chopped fresh ginger, and honey

- 1 teaspoon sea salt

- 2 garlic cloves, chopped

- 1 teaspoon red pepper flakes, crushed

- 1/4 cup olive oil

For the salad:

- 1/2 cup shredded carrots

- 4 ounces baby spring mix lettuce

- 1/2 cup cucumber, thinly sliced

- 1/4 cup each of chopped fresh basil, sliced green onions, and chopped fresh cilantro leaves

- 1/2 cup sliced each yellow and red bell peppers

Directions:

1. Prepare the Thai peanut dressing. Put the following in a food processor with a metal blade attachment: soy sauce, red pepper flakes, ginger, salt, oil, vinegar, peanut butter, garlic, honey, mint leaves, and lime juice. Process until smooth.

2. Put 3/4 cup of the dressing and shrimp inside a Zip-loc bag. Seal the bag and leave to marinate for 30 minutes. Put the shrimp on 4 skewers. Cook on a pre-heated grill for 8 minutes. Transfer to a plate and allow to cool.

3. Arrange the salad ingredients on a plate. Drizzle with the remaining dressing and top with the grilled shrimp before serving.

Seeds and Greens Salad

Yield: 6 servings

Ingredients:

- 1 teaspoon Herbes de Provence

- 2 cups butternut squash, diced

- 1 cup pomegranate seeds

- 1 tablespoon olive oil

- 1/2 cup feta cheese, crumbled

- 1/4 cup toasted pumpkin seeds

- 4 cups mixed leafy greens

For the balsamic dressing:

- 2 teaspoons Dijon mustard

- 1/2 teaspoon sea salt

- 2 garlic cloves

- 1/4 teaspoon freshly ground black pepper

- 1/2 cup olive oil

- 1/4 cup balsamic vinegar

- 1 teaspoon Herbes de Provence

- 1 tablespoon agave nectar

Directions:

1. Put the butternut squash on a baking sheet and spread all over. Sprinkle Herbes de Provence and olive oil on top. Toss to coat. Roast in a preheated

oven at 425 degrees for 15 minutes. Flip them and continue roasting for 15 more minutes. Place on a wire rack to cool.

2. Put the mixed greens in a bowl. Add the pumpkin seeds, pomegranate seeds, feta cheese, and roasted squash.

3. Put all the ingredients for the dressing in a food processor. Process until smooth. Pour this over the salad. Gently mix before serving.

22 - Gastric Sleeve Diet Main Dish Recipes

Baked Pork Chops with Fruity Slaw

Yield: 4 servings

Ingredients:

- 4 center cut pork chops

- Cooking spray

- 1/2 cup low-fat evaporated canned milk

- 1/2 teaspoon garlic powder

- 1 tablespoon olive oil

- Sea salt and freshly ground black pepper to taste

- 1/2 cup Italian seasoned breadcrumbs

For the apple pear slaw:

- 1 pear, grated

- 1 apple, grated

- 2 tablespoons low-sugar apricot preserves

Directions:

1. Put the milk in a shallow dish. In another shallow dish, mix the garlic, salt, pepper, and breadcrumbs.

2. Dip the meat in the milk until all sides are covered. Dredge it in the bread crumb mixture until evenly coated. Do this with all the pieces of meat.

3. Heat oil in a pan over medium-high flame. Cook the breaded pork chop until all sides are browned. Transfer the browned pork chops on a greased baking sheet. Bake in a preheated oven at 350 degrees for 30 minutes.

4. Put the baked meat on a plate. Pour the extra juices on top. Loosely cover with foil and leave for 5 minutes to rest.

5. Combine all the ingredients for the slaw. Put a spoonful of the slaw at the top of each pork chop before serving.

Slow Cooker Pulled Pork

Yield: 10 servings

Ingredients:

- 1 cup chicken broth

- 1 onion, thinly sliced

- 2 teaspoons sea salt

- 3 garlic cloves, thinly sliced

- 1/2 teaspoon each of ground cinnamon and ground cumin

- 1 boneless pork roast

- 1 tablespoon each of chili powder and brown sugar

- 2 cups barbecue sauce

Directions:

1. Arrange the garlic and onion in a single layer at the bottom of the slow cooker. Add the broth.

2. In a bowl, mix the cinnamon, salt, cumin, chili powder, and sugar. Generously rub the pork with the mixture. Put the meat in the slow cooker. Close the lid and cook for up to 6 hours on a high setting.

3. Transfer the cooked meat to a bowl. Strain the cooking liquid from the slow cooker. Add the solid particles to the meat. Set aside the strained liquid.

4. Shred the meat and discard excess fat. Add the sauce and mix well.

This is best served with baked potato sweet fries or coleslaw.

Bacon and Beef Stew

Yield: 8 servings

Ingredients:

- 5 cups beef broth, divided

- 5 bacon slices, sliced into small pieces

- 1/2 cup flour

- 3 pounds sirloin beef, sliced into cubes

- 3 garlic cloves, minced

- 1 onion, cut into wedges

- 1 teaspoon each of thyme, oregano, and rosemary

- 2 tablespoons tomato paste

- Sea salt and freshly ground pepper to taste

- 1/2 pound carrots, rinsed and sliced diagonally

- 1 pound whole mushrooms, quartered

- 2 bay leaves

- 3 celery ribs, rinsed and sliced

- 1 pound potatoes, rinsed and cut into cubes

Directions:

1. Put the flour in a shallow dish and dredge the meat until evenly coated.

2. Put the bacon in a soup pot over medium-high heat. Cook until crisp. Transfer to a plate lined with paper towels. Sear the coated meat in the bacon drippings until all sides are browned. Transfer to another plate.

3. Saute the garlic, onion, celery, and carrots in the same soup pot. Cook for 5 minutes before adding the beef broth. Scrape the bits at the bottom of the pot using a metal spatula. Bring to a boil. Stir in the tomato paste. Add the potato, mushrooms, bay leaves, rosemary, oregano, thyme, cooked beef and bacon, and the rest of the beef broth. Bring to a boil. Turn the heat to low and cover the pot. Simmer for 2 hours while occasionally stirring.

4. Remove the bay leaves and season with salt and pepper before serving.

Zucchini Lasagna

Yield: 8 servings

Ingredients:

- 1 6-ounce can tomato paste

- 1 15-ounce can Italian stewed tomatoes

- 2 1/2 cups zucchini, sliced lengthwise

- 1/2 cup onion, chopped

- 1/4 cup water

- 1 tablespoon each of chopped fresh oregano and chopped fresh basil leaves

- 1 pound extra-lean ground beef

- 1 egg

- 2 garlic cloves, minced

- Cooking spray

- Sea salt and freshly ground black pepper to taste

- 1/4 cup shaved Parmesan cheese

- 1 cup low-fat ricotta cheese

- 2 tablespoons chopped fresh Italian-leaf parsley

- 1 cup shredded mozzarella cheese, divided

Directions:

1. Cook the zucchinis and transfer to a plate lined with paper towels to remove excess moisture.

2. Put the meat, garlic, and onions in a pan over medium-high heat. Cook until the meat is browned on all sides. Drain the fat. Add basil, tomato paste, water, oregano, and tomatoes. Season with salt and pepper. Stir to combine and bring to a boil. Turn the heat to low and simmer for 2 minutes.

3. In a bowl, mix the beaten egg, parsley, 1/2 cup of shredded mozzarella cheese, and ricotta cheese.

4. Put 1/3 of the meat mixture on the bottom of a greased baking dish. Top with half of the zucchini slices. Add half of the ricotta cheese mixture. Add the rest of the ingredients following the same sequence. Bake in a preheated oven at 375 degrees for 30 minutes. Spread the rest of the mozzarella and parmesan cheese on top. Bake for another 10 minutes. Leave for 10 minutes before serving.

Grilled Tilapia with Papaya Salsa

Yield: 4 servings

Ingredients:

- 4 4 ounce tilapia fillets

- 1/4 cup extra-virgin olive oil

- 1 lemon, juiced

- 1 garlic clove, minced

- Sea salt and freshly ground black pepper to taste

- 2 tablespoons each of chopped fresh basil and chopped fresh Italian parsley

For the papaya salsa:

- 1 fresh lime, juiced

- 1/2 cup red onion, diced

- 1/2 cup red bell pepper, cubed

- 1/2 cup fresh cilantro, chopped

- 1 papaya, diced

- 1 jalapeno pepper, seeded and minced

Directions:

1. In a bowl, mix the lemon juice, olive oil, salt, pepper, basil, parsley, and garlic. Transfer to a Ziploc bag. Add the fish fillets. Seal the bag and marinate for an hour.

2. Put all the ingredients for the salsa, except for the papaya, in the food processor. Process until chopped. Transfer to a bowl and fold in the diced papaya.

3. Drain excess liquid from the tilapia fillets. Cook on a preheated and lightly oiled grill for 4 minutes on each side.

4. Serve the tilapia fillets with the papaya salsa on the side.

Tuna Casserole with Cheese

Yield: 6 servings

Ingredients:

- 3 6-ounce cans tuna, drained and flaked

- 1 tablespoon each of diced onion and butter

- 1/2 cup frozen petite green peas

- 2 tablespoons each of light mayonnaise and chopped celery

- 1/4 teaspoon black pepper

- 1/2 teaspoon salt

- 1 cup reduced-fat cheddar cheese, shredded

- 1/2 teaspoon garlic powder

- 1/3 cup reduced-fat cream cheese

Directions:

1. Melt butter in a pan over medium-high heat. Saute the onion and celery for 3 minutes.

2. Transfer the cooked celery and onion to a bowl. Add mayonnaise, tuna, green peas, salt, pepper, cream cheese, and garlic powder. Mix well. Transfer to a casserole dish. Top with cheese. Bake in a preheated oven at 375 degrees for 20 minutes. Leave to rest for 5 minutes before serving.

Salmon Burgers

Yield: 4

Ingredients:

- 1 pound salmon fillets, skinned and minced

- 1 egg, lightly beaten

- 1/4 cup each of red and yellow bell pepper, diced

- 1 garlic clove, minced

- 1/4 teaspoons salt

- 1/4 cup panko crumbs

- 2 teaspoons soy sauce

- Cooking spray

- 2 tablespoons chopped onion

- 1/2 teaspoons fresh lemon juice

For the lemon basil mayonnaise:

- 1 teaspoon Dijon mustard

- 2 garlic cloves, minced

- 1/2 cup light mayonnaise

- 1/2 teaspoon lemon pepper

- 1 teaspoon fresh lemon juice

- 1 teaspoon dried basil

Directions:

1. In a bowl, mix the salmon, peppers, garlic, and

panko. In another bowl, mix salt, soy sauce, lemon juice, and egg. Combine the 2 mixtures. Use your hands to form 4 patties.

2. Lightly grease a skillet over medium-high heat. Cook each side of the patty for 5 minutes.

3. Combine all the ingredients for the lemon basil mayonnaise in a bowl.

4. Serve the patties along with the mayo.

Pesto Fish Roll-Ups

Yield: 4 servings

Ingredients:

- 4 4-ounce fish fillets, such as cod or flounder

- 1 tablespoon olive oil

- 1/4 cup shredded carrot

- 1/4 cup basil pesto

- Cooking spray

- 2 garlic cloves, minced

- Sea salt and freshly ground black pepper to taste

- 2 tablespoons panko breadcrumbs

- 1/4 cup finely chopped pecans

- 1/2 teaspoons lemon zest

Directions:

1. Rinse the fillets and pat them dry. Spread one side with 1 tablespoon of basil pesto. Sprinkle a tablespoon of shredded carrot on top. Roll up the fish and secure the ends with toothpicks. Arrange them in an oiled baking dish. Lightly brush with olive oil.

2. In a bowl, mix the lemon zest, panko bread crumbs, pecans, salt, pepper, and garlic. Press the mixture on top of the fish roll-ups. Bake in a preheated oven at 375 degrees for 25 minutes.

Spaghetti Squash

Yield: 6 servings

Ingredients:

- 2 tomatoes, diced

- 2 pounds spaghetti squash, halved and seeded

- 1 zucchini, diced

- Sea salt and freshly ground black pepper to taste

- 2 tablespoons olive oil, divided

- 1/2 cup shaved Parmesan cheese

- 1/2 red onion, thinly sliced

- 1/4 cup fresh basil leaves, chopped and divided

- 2 garlic cloves, minced

Directions:

1. Arrange the squash with the cut sides facing down in a baking dish. Pour 1/4 cup of water and cover. Microwave for 12 minutes on a high setting.

2. Heat a tablespoon of olive oil in a skillet over me-

dium-high flame. Cook the garlic and onion for 3 minutes. Stir in the zucchini and cook for 3 more minutes. Add 2 tablespoons of basil leaves, tomatoes, and season with salt and pepper. Turn the heat to low and simmer for 10 minutes.

3. Scrape the strands of squash to a bowl. Add the rest of the olive oil and toss to coat. Drizzle with the vegetable mixture on top. Garnish with cheese and the rest of the basil leaves before serving.

Caribbean Chicken

Yield: 6 servings

Ingredients:

- 1 pound chicken tenders

- 1/2 cup honey

- 1 tablespoon butter

- 1/4 cup currants

- 1/4 cup minced onion

- 1/4 cup Dijon mustard

- 1/4 cup mango chutney

- 2 garlic cloves, minced

- 1/2 teaspoon salt

- 1 teaspoon curry powder

Directions:

1. Melt butter in a pan over medium-high flame. Saute the garlic and onion for 2 minutes. Add the meat and cook until all sides are browned.

2. In a bowl, mix the mustard, honey, salt, curry, currants, and chutney. Pour this over the meat and stir. Cover the pan. Turn the heat to medium and simmer for 10 minutes.

23 - Conclusion

Thank you again for buying this book!

I hope this book was able to help you to easily cope with your life after the gastric sleeve surgery. I hope that this book also gives you ideas on what to eat and how to prepare different dishes that will fit your new dietary requirements.

Book 3 - Weight Loss Surgery Cookbook

Perfect Bariatric-Friendly Recovery Diet After Gastric Bypass (Lifelong Eating, Puree, Maintain Weight Loss, Skinny)

1 - Introduction

I want to thank you and congratulate you for buying this book.

This book contains proven steps and strategies on how to understand what to do after undergoing gastric bypass surgery. This contains information that will help you in coping with the changes and in learning what to do as the healing process progresses.

This book has a wide variety of recipes that are suited for every stage of the healing process. This teaches you about meals and dishes that you can come up with in order to maintain weight loss and make sure that you will benefit from the process for a long time.

Thanks again for buying this book, I hope you enjoy it!

2 - An Overview about the Gastric Bypass Surgery

Known as the most invasive weight loss procedure, the gastric bypass surgery offers the most efficient technique to losing weight. This is ideal for people who are obese or overweight with above 40 Body Mass Index or BMI. Patients at this rate are tagged as morbidly obese.

They are likely suffering from weight-related health problems, which include sleep apnea, high blood pressure, and type 2 diabetes. If you are at this point in your life, the surgery will not only help you lose weight to look good and feel better about yourself but most importantly, it can improve your health and the quality or your life.

The procedure creates a new stomach pouch that is the same size as an egg or a golf ball. A smaller pouch will limit the amount of food that you can take. With a smaller stomach, you will feel less hungry and would only crave to eat smaller portions. The surgery attaches a part of the small intestine to the new pouch.

This allows food to bypass most of the small intestine. As a result, the body absorbs a limited amount of nutrients and calories. This is the main cause of the weight loss – the food that you eat is absorbed less readily by the body.

Before the surgery, your medical team will ask you to follow a pre-operative diet to reduce the size of your liver. The operation is life-changing. Once done, you will modify your dietary habits to last a lifetime. Your surgeon will advise you to follow a staged gastric bypass diet. You will begin with a full liquid diet and it will gradually progress until you are on a normal diet.

Through the dietary changes, your medical team will guide you and tell you when it is safe to progress. They will also give you supplements and medications to make the process of healing faster. You will also be given vitamins, supplements, and minerals that you can take for the rest of your life.

It is important to remember that since your body will be taking in fewer calories, you have to choose the right food to eat in order to maintain a healthy and balanced diet.

3 - The Healing Process

It will take up to 8 weeks for your pouch to completely heal. Planning your meals is important. Your goal is not only to lose weight but also to keep your lean body mass or muscles. Each meal must contain high amounts of protein and low amounts of sugar and fat.

After the operation, your pouch is like that of a baby and it can only absorb liquid and pureed items during the first weeks. This is the purpose of this book – so that you would know what to eat depending on what level you are in.

As you progress in the diet, you can still eat the food items from the previous stages. Whenever you find it hard to tolerate a food item, eliminate it first from your diet for a couple of weeks before reintroducing it to your daily diet.

The Mindful Eating Technique

You will apply this eating technique before and after the surgery. Be always mindful not only of what you eat but how you do it. Consume your food at least 30 minutes or longer, especially in the first weeks following the surgery. Take your time in chewing your food to a liquid consistency. You must also drink slowly.

Do not finish your food if your body already feels full. Put the food away immediately before you get tempted to have another bite.

Helping Yourself Heal Faster

Your dietitian will guide you throughout the process to make it easier for you to make the right food choices. He/she will address your needs after your pouch has thoroughly healed and you are on the last stage of the diet by giving you the nutritional guidelines that you need to follow for the rest of your life.

Here are some important points that you need to remember

The procedure will create an impact and big changes in your life. The struggle is not only physical but also emotional and mental. There are times when you will feel fat even though you are not. It is normal to feel anxious, especially when you hear people's comments about the changes in you.

Always remember that you are not alone in the journey. Join post-operative support groups because they will help a lot in making you more emotionally stable. You must also never lose communication with your medical team. Tell them about your progress and ask for their advice whenever you are going through something that you don't understand.

Help keep the weight off, build and maintain your muscle mass by exercising. Get the approval of your clinician before participating in resistance and cardiovascular training. If you are still not allowed to perform these exercises, opt for simple exercises like walking.

Losing weight is like a plight to a staircase. There are times when it will slow down and times when you will experience plateaus. If the plateau happens for more than 2 weeks, track your exercise and record what you eat. You can adjust your diet and exercise and see if there is any improvement.

If it lasts for more than 4 weeks, get the help of your dietitian and show to him/her your diet and exercise records. Never compare yourself to others who have undergone the same process. Different people will lose weight at different rates.

Here are some of the nutrition considerations following your gastric bypass operation

Maintain a daily fluid intake of 64 ounces or more, depending on your dietary requirement. This will keep your body hydrated by replacing the lost fluids as you lose weight. Separate the fluids from your meals by half an hour. Do not drink while eating a regular meal because the fluids will fill your pouch faster.

Know your daily protein requirement and always meet your protein goals. This helps in the healing process and in preserving your body muscles.

Always follow the mindful eating process. Take tiny bites, eat slowly and eat small frequent meals.

There are instances when you will experience the Dumping syndrome. This happens after eating high sugary and high-fat foods. The symptoms are similar to flu, such as sweating, nausea, diarrhea, and vomiting. These symptoms typically last for 30 minutes. You can avoid experiencing these symptoms by eating foods with around 3 to 5 grams of fat and 14 grams of sugar or less per serving.

There are certain patients who experience hair loss after the surgery. Lack of vitamins and proteins in the diet usually cause this problem. This is also how your body reacts to rapid weight loss. Tell your dietitian if you are experiencing hair loss so that he/she can adjust your vitamins and protein intake. This problem is temporary and the hair grows back normally again after 3 to 6 months.

It is also common to experience a honeymoon period after the operation. It is normal to lack appetite but never make it an excuse to skip meals. You need to meet your daily nutritional requirement and always follow the diet plan of 4 to 6 small meals per day.

Your food preferences may vary as you develop changes in taste.

Many patients experience lactose intolerance after the surgery characterized by diarrhea, cramping, bloating or gas. These are symptoms that you have developed lactose intolerance from the sugar found in milk. Tell your dietitian so that he/she can design a lactose-free diet. This issue will naturally resolve in 3 to 6 months.

Keep records of your meals each day. These logs will help you keep track of the time and frequency of your meals, and what you have eaten.

You need to go to your doctor whenever it is time for a follow-up and check-up. Your labs have to be tested periodically to check if you are not lacking nutrients and vitamins. After the surgery, the most common deficiencies that you are at risk of include Vitamin D, B12, Iron, and Folate.

4 - Dietary Stages after Undergoing Gastric Bypass Surgery

Life after the operation won't be a breeze. You are in a healing process and it will only succeed with your full cooperation. Always remember that your diet will change drastically. You will eventually have the chance to grab a bite or two of your favorite dish, but before that day comes, you need to religiously follow what's allowed to eat depending on the healing phase that you are in.

This book contains a detailed guide about the dietary stages following your gastric bypass surgery.

5 - The First Period: The Fluid Phase

This period refers to the first two weeks following the surgery. The diet aims to help the surgical wounds and the sutures between the small intestines and stomach heal at a faster rate. At this point, you cannot eat too fast or too heavy.

The sutures are still fragile. Eating foods that are unsuitable for this period of the healing process can lead to rupture of the sutures, which can cause the leakage of the contents of your intestines into the abdominal cavity.

Listen to your body. Stop eating once you feel any pain and discomfort even if you feel like you are still not full. This is the body's signal that it has already eaten enough.

Day 1

After the surgery, you are only allowed to consume 1 ounce of water every hour. You will drink from a medicine cup. You have to sip the water in a slow manner. Stop drinking if it makes you feel sick. You will be given swabs to moisten your dry mouth, which is typical to happen at this point.

Day 2

You are still in the hospital at this point. You will be allowed to consume clear liquids one day after the surgery. You can consume 3 ounces of bouillon and/or sugar-free gelatin thrice a day. You can sip plain water or a flat diet ginger ale in between your meals. Your goal is to sip up to 4 ounces of fluid per hour in between your meals.

Aside from nutrition, it is important that you walk as much as you can, not unless your doctor advises you against it. Have a family member or a nurse assist you all the time to ensure your safety.

Day 3 Onwards

After Day 2, you will follow a high-protein full liquid diet. You will do this for 2 weeks. Your goal is to take in at least 64 ounces of fluids per day. Your protein intake per day must be 50 to 60 grams for women and 60 to 70 grams for men and women who are taller than 5'8". Aim for 400 to 600 kilocalorie per day.

You have to eat and sip in a slow manner. Stop at once when

your body feels sick or it tells you that it is full. Make sure that you can suck your drinks using a straw and they do not contain lumps and bits. Never gulp your drinks or else you might feel nauseated or even vomit. To avoid dehydration, you must consume at least 2.5 liters per day, most of which are nutritious liquids.

Here are some samples of the healthy liquids and the required amount that you can take at this stage:

- 1 to 2 small glasses of unsweetened fruit juice

- Slimfast

- 1 to 2 tablespoons of skimmed milk for every 200 ml of water. You can also use semi-skimmed milk fortified with skimmed milk powder

- Tinned or homemade smooth soup fortified with up to 2 tablespoons of skimmed milk powder.

- Supplements, which include Complan and Build-Up, which are suitable for diabetics

- Homemade smoothies

You can take coffee, water, tea or squash, but take them in addition to and not in replacement of any healthy liquids in the list above.

A typical meal plan within this period includes 200 ml of fruit juice for breakfast, 200 ml of homemade smoothie in mid-morning, 200 ml of Slimfast for lunch, Build-Up or Complan or 200 ml dilution of skimmed milk in mid-afternoon, 200 ml of Complan or Build-Up for Dinner and 200 ml of fortified soup for a late-night snack. You can take other liquids in between.

You have to practice listening to what your stomach is telling you. Take your time in eating or in this case, in sipping your meals. You can allow up to 30 minutes for each meal. Listen to your stomach and stop eating when it is full.

This comes with the feeling of pressure at the back of the sternum and under the ribcage. You may also feel nauseous, especially during the first week, pain in the stomach region and on the upper part of thorax or shoulder.

It is important that you do not overfill your pouch. This will make the surgery useless. Eating more than what's required will stretch the pouch, which can lead to complications. To be safe, make sure that you are always mindful of what and you are not eating. If you don't feel an empty stomach, set a reminder so that you won't forget to eat on schedule.

- Here is the food that you have to avoid at this stage:

- Fruits and veggies that are tough and raw

- Rice

- Solid food that is not pureed

- Yogurt with big chunks of fruits

- Peas

- Pasta and noodles

- Corn

- Candies and sweets

- Red meat

- Ice cream

- Chunky peanut butter

- Bread

Here is the food that you can gradually incorporate into your diet. Try these one at a time. If you don't feel good about them, drop them from the list and put them back after several days. If your stomach finds it hard to tolerate pureed food, go back to taking clear liquids.

Pureed vegetables, such as green beans, carrots, cauliflower, beetroot, and broccoli.

Vegetable juice and tomato juice

Pureed low-fat casserole or stew with soft vegetables

Pureed apple or peaches

Mashed banana

Minced pork or turkey

Pureed salmon, tuna, white fish or herring

1 egg yolk and egg white

Pureed soups and cream soups

Pudding and yogurt with low-sugar content

Pureed lean turkey or chicken

6 - Liquid Consumption

Make sure that you drink more than 1.2 liters of liquid per day. Drink more, especially when your urine begins to develop a foul smell and when it becomes dark and cloudy. The color of your urine has to be pale yellow. Sip the liquids slowly and take them separately from your meals.

You can take them 30 mins before and after a meal. It is not advisable to drink using a straw. You will swallow more air when you use a straw, which can lead to belching that will cause pain in the upper thorax and shoulder.

Avoid carbonated drinks and anything that contains too much sugar. Anything that has more than 20 grams of sugar for every 240 ml may cause dumping syndrome, which symptoms include spasmodic pain, dizziness, nausea, and flushing. It is important that you keep a bottle of water with you all the time. This way, it won't be difficult to remember to drink often in a slow manner to avoid dehydration.

Here's a list of the allowed drinks in this phase:

- Water

- Ice cubes

- Non-carbonated flavored water

- Juices diluted in water

- Protein-loaded fruit drinks

- Decaffeinated tea

- Decaffeinated coffee (drink it when warm and not hot)

- Sugar-free popsicles

- Power Aid Zero

- Fat-free and low sodium broth

Here are the drinks that you ought to avoid:

- Carbonated drinks

- Soft drinks

- Drinks with sweet sugar

- Sports drinks

Preparing Your Own Smoothies

Your smoothies must have a watery consistency. Aside from the fruits, each preparation must contain flavorings, liquid, and protein. You can use any fruits – fresh, conserved or frozen. If you want the drink to be thicker, use frozen fruits or add ice cubes when using fresh fruits.

For the liquid, you can choose from soymilk, milk, and protein drink. If you don't like to add the latter, you can instead put 50 ml of yogurt, cottage or ricotta cheese to the mixture. For flavorings, you can use salt, ginger, parsley, cinnamon, dill, cardamom, parsley, and clove. Experiment on the taste by first adding 1/8 teaspoonful of the flavor. Add more according to taste.

Here are some samples of the smoothie mixtures that you can concoct:

- 25 ml each of milk, tofu, and mashed pineapple, ice cubes, and 1/8 teaspoon of ginger

- 25 ml each of cottage cheese and pureed frozen berry mix, 1/8 teaspoon of crushed nutmeg, and 50 ml of protein drink

- 25 ml each of vanilla-flavored yogurt and pureed frozen peaches, 1/8 teaspoon of cinnamon, and 50 ml of protein drink

7 - Allowed Vitamins and Medicines

- Omeprazole tablets. You will be given a prescription for the tablets that you will take for 4 weeks.

- Multivitamin. Start taking 1 tablet two times a day from the second postoperative week.

- Vitamin B12 replacement therapy with injections. This will be administered once every 3 months. The first shot will be given before getting discharged from the hospital.

- Clexane injection once daily for 10 days.

Physical Activity

Make sure that you don't lift more than 6 kilos of weight. Move as much as you can as soon as possible after undergoing the procedure. Your body easily gets tired due to the decreased daily consumption of calories. Rest if you must but go walking whenever you can. You can make the trek more difficult to challenge yourself, such as walking on an uneven surface or walking up and down the stairs.

Other Diet Tips for this Phase

You will lose weight because of the dramatic decrease in your caloric intake. This is why it is important to choose products that are sugar-free or labeled as with no sugar added.

- There are times when you will experience dry mouth even after you have consumed the daily fluid requirement. This is a sign of dehydration and that you need to drink more.

- Do not forget to take or inject the prescription medications that you were given upon your release from the hospital.

- Get in touch with your medical team for any pain and other problems that are causing too much inconvenience.

Meeting the Daily Protein Requirement

Here's a detailed list of the food choices at this stage and how much protein and calories they contain per serving.

- 8 ounces of ready to drink Carnation Instant Breakfast with no sugar added contain 13 grams of protein and 150 calories

- 8 ounces of skim milk with Carnation Instant Breakfast with no sugar added contain 13 grams of protein and 150 calories

- 8 ounces of ready to drink Slimfast contain 10 to 20 grams of protein and 220 to 180 calories

- 11 ounces of ready to drink EAS AdvantEdge contain 17 grams of protein and 110 calories

- 8 ounces of Lactaid skim milk contains 8 grams of protein and 80 calories

- 8 ounces of Simple Smart fat-free milk contains 10 grams of protein and 90 calories

- 8 ounces of skim milk contains 8 grams of protein and 90 calories

- 2 egg whites contain 8 grams of protein and 34 calories

- 1/2 cup of scrambled liquid egg substitute contains 12 grams of protein and 60 calories

- 1/4 cup of fat-free ricotta cheese contains 6 to 10 grams of protein and 40 to 80 calories

- 1/2 cup of fat-free or 1 percent of cottage cheese contains 13 to 14 grams of protein and 70 to 80 calories

- 6 to 8 ounces of light yogurt contain 5 to 8 grams of protein and 60 to 120 calories

- Low-fat or fat-free cream soups mixed with 8 ounces of skim milk contain 10 grams of protein and 190 calories

- 1/2 cup of fat-free or sugar-free instant pudding contains 4 to 5 grams of protein and 75 to 100 calories

Sample Meal Plan

Here's a meal plan that will yield 59 grams of protein, 530 calories, and 56 ounces of fluids:

Begin your day by taking your fluids from 7 to 7:30. In this sample, consume 12 ounces of water. From 8 to 9:00 in the morning, consume your first meal, which is 8 ounces of light yogurt. Take your fluids, 12 ounces of crystal light, from 9:30 to 11:30. Consume your 2nd meal, which is Slim Fast, from 12 noon to 1:00. Take your fluids again, 8 ounces of water, from 1:30 to 3:00.

Take your third meal, 1/2 cup of egg beaters, from 3:30 to 4:00. From 4:30 to 6:00, take your fluids, which is 24 ounces of Power Aid Zero. You will consume your 4th meal from 6:30 to 7:30, which is sugar-free Jello pudding. The last meal of the day is 1/2 cup of cottage cheese that should be eaten from 9:00 to 9:30.

As you can see, everything is monitored, including the amount of time that you will spend consuming each meal. Always take it slow, from 30 to 45 minutes. This will make it easier for your pouch to absorb the foods and all the nutrients that they contain.

8 - First Phase Recipes

Always remember that you can only take blended fruits and veggies, and mix with shakes.

Wild Berry Boost

Place the following ingredients in a blender:

- 8 blueberries

- 4 strawberries

- 4 raspberries

- 1/2 cup of ice cubes

- 8 ounces of non-fat milk

- 2 scoops of vanilla flavored protein powder

Process all the ingredients until smooth and free of lumps. Transfer to a glass and serve.

The Hulk

Here are the ingredients needed to make this smoothie:

- 8 ounces of low-fat milk or cold water

- 3 ice cubes

- 1/2 tablespoon of sugar-free pistachio pudding mix

- A few drops of peppermint extract or 1 mint leaf

- 2 scoops of vanilla protein powder

Process all the ingredients in a blender until smooth. You can opt to add a drop or 2 of green food coloring to the mixture.

Pumpkin Pie Shake

Blend the following ingredients until smooth:

- 1 cup of ice cubes

- 1 cup of soy milk or skim milk

- 1/4 cup of pumpkin puree

- 1 scoop of vanilla protein powder

- 1/4 cup of vanilla yogurt

- 1/2 teaspoon of pumpkin pie spice

- 2 tablespoons of Splenda granular

Mocha Proticcino

Here are the needed ingredients to make this mix:

- 8 ounces of skim milk

- 1 tablespoon of decaf instant coffee

- 1 scoop of vanilla or chocolate protein powder

Put all the ingredients in a blender and process until smooth. You can tweak the recipe by adding 1/4 banana. Blend until free of lumps. Another way to tweak this is by adding 2 teaspoons of low-sugar peanut butter.

Cinnamon Roll Protein Shake

Put the following ingredients in a blender and process until smooth and free of lumps:

- 1/4 teaspoon of cinnamon

- 1 scoop of vanilla protein powder

- 3 ice cubes

- 1 tablespoon of sugar-free instant vanilla pudding

- 8 ounces of low-fat milk or water

- A dash or two of butter-flavored extract or sprinkles

- 1/4 teaspoon of vanilla extract

- 1 packet of Splenda

Apple Cinnamon

Blend all the ingredients in a blender until smooth:

- 1 teaspoon of cinnamon

- 2 scoops of vanilla whey protein powder

- 1 cup of chopped frozen apple

- 1 1/2 cups of skim milk or water

High-Protein Pudding

To prepare this, you will need a 4-serving package of the uncooked Jell-O sugar-free instant pudding.

Mix 2 scoops of unflavored protein powder and 2 cups of cold skim milk. Shake to mix well. Prepare the Jell-O sugar-free instant pudding according to package directions. Add the milk and protein powder mixture. Mix thoroughly. Chill and serve.

After two weeks, you will need to see your medical team to assess your progress. It is up to your dietitian whether it is safe for you to progress to the next phase of the diet or not. He/she will base the decision on the findings of your doctor.

9 - The Second Period: Soft and Moist Protein Diet

This period covers the third and fourth week after your surgery. For some, this can last up to 6 weeks. It really depends on how your stomach is recuperating and how your whole system is adjusting to the new scheme of things. At this phase, you will have more options of foods to eat.

This is to prepare your stomach for solid food. Your pouch is gradually recovering but it is still not capable of digesting solid food. The food choices that you have during this phase only require minimal chewing.

Your goal is to take in more than 64 ounces of fluids per day. Your protein intake per day is 50 to 60 grams for women and 60 to 70 grams for men and women who are taller than 5'8". Aim for 550 to 700 kilocalorie per day.

At this stage, it is no longer necessary to puree your foods. Mash your foods to make them chewable and do not swallow large chunks. Introduce food items one at a time to check if you can tolerate them. If not, remove them from the diet and try eating them again after a week.

Train yourself to eat 3 to 5 small regular meals a day. Continuous nibbling during the day is not advisable because it reduces weight loss. Eat slowly and chew your food thoroughly.

Eating fast may lead to vomiting and the Dumping syndrome. Initially, the connections between the small intestine and stomach are narrow. By eating slowly, the connections guarantee a smooth movement of the food that passes through them.

Always feel the pressure at the back of your sternum beneath the ribcage. This means that you are full and it can happen even after eating 2 to 3 mouthfuls. Monitor the amount of protein that you take all the time. You can consume protein additives if you are finding it hard to meet the required amount from your regular meals.

Here are the foods that you have to avoid at this stage:

- Red meat

- Tough, dry, and hard meat

- Chunky peanut butter

- Fried egg

- Raw fruits with tough skin

- Hard fruits

- Ice cream

- Chewing gum and other sweets

- White bread

- Soft half-baked bread

- Broccoli stems

- Fresh asparagus

- Fats and sugars

Here are the foods allowed to eat in this phase:

- Fruits and vegetables without seeds and soft-boiled husks

- Soft fresh fruits

- Soft and juicy lean meat

- Low-fat cottage cheese

- Fish

- Eggs

- Soft tofu

- Porridges with milk

- Pretzels

- Soft vegetables and fruits conserved in on juice

- Low-fat yogurt

Liquid Consumption

Sip liquids in the same manner as you did in the previous phase. The required amount of fluid intake per day is 1.2 to 1.5 liters. Do not drink half an hour before eating a regular meal. Your stomach has to be empty when you eat. You are also not allowed to drink while eating.

This will fill up your pouch fast, which can lead to experiencing the Dumping syndrome, nausea, abdominal pain, and vomiting. Wait 30 minutes or more after eating a meal before drinking liquids. This aims to avoid fast flushing of the food in your stomach.

Here's a list of the allowed drinks to take in this phase:

- Water

- Non-carbonated flavored water

- Juices diluted in water

- Sugar-free tea

Here are the drinks that you ought to avoid:

- Carbonated drinks

- Soft drinks

- Drinks with sweet sugar

- Sports drinks

Allowed Vitamins and Medicines

- Continue taking Omeprazole tablets and Multivitamin

- Vitamin B12 replacement therapy with injections

- 30 microgram D3-vitamin tablet once per day

- 600-milligram Calcium nitrate tablets twice a day beginning on the 3rd day after the surgery

- 100-milligram of iron preparations once every other day for women in fertile age

Physical Activity

It is important to remain as physically active as possible. You can ride a bike, perform Nordic walking, speed walking, or simply walk at times when you are not in the mood to do more than that. You are not allowed to lift more than 6 kilos of heavy objects. You can go swimming 3 weeks after the operation.

Other Diet Tips for this Phase

- Cut your food to a ground consistency. Add sugar-free and fat-free condiments to keep them moist. You can also cook them in ways that they will retain the moisture, such as roasting, baking, poaching, and steaming.

- Since you will be eating your food slowly, you can keep them warm by placing your plate on a baby food warmer tray.

- After cooking your meal, weigh it using a food scale. Aim for about 3 ounces of protein per meal.

- Avoid chewing gum. If you accidentally swallow it, the gum will block the connection to your pouch.

- If you are always meeting your daily protein goals, you can include half a cup of mashed vegetables or mashed potatoes mixed with skim milk to your daily menu and have it once a day.

- If you are often experiencing constipation, add a fiber

supplement to your fluids.

Meeting the Daily Protein Requirement

Here's a detailed list of the food choices at this stage and how much protein and calories they contain per serving.

Vegetarian protein sources:

- 1/2 cup of scrambled liquid egg substitute contains 12 grams of protein and 60 calories

- 2 tablespoons of hummus contain 8 grams of protein and 100 calories

- 1/2 cup of beans, such as refried, black and kidney beans, contains 8 grams of protein and 103 calories

- 3 ounces of fat-free or low-fat cheese contain 20 grams of protein and 124 calories

- 1 large egg contains 6 grams of protein and 78 calories

- 1/2 cup of fat-free or 1 percent cottage cheese contains 15 grams of protein and 80 calories

- 1/2 cup of lentils contains 9 grams of protein and 115 calories

- 1/2 cup of ground soy crumbles contains 11 grams of protein and 70 calories

- 1/2 cup of tempeh contains 16 grams of protein and 165 calories

- 1/2 cup of tofu contains 20 grams of protein and 183 calories

- 1 vegetable burger patty contains 9 grams of protein and 70 calories

Animal protein sources:

- 2.5 ounces of baby food contains 8 grams of protein and 50 calories

- 3 ounces of ground meat contain 21 to 23 grams of protein and 150 calories

- 1/2 cup of turkey chili contains 8 grams of protein and 92 calories

- 3 ounces of canned chicken breast packed in water contain 16 grams of protein and 80 calories

- 3 ounces of fish, such as sole, halibut, and haddock contain 21 to 23 grams of protein and 90 to 120 calories

- 3 ounces of fatty fish like bluefish and salmon contain 21 to 23 grams of protein and 160 calories

- 3 ounces of tuna packed in water contain 20 to 22 grams of protein and 100 to 110 calories

- 3 ounces of scallops, shrimp, and crabmeat contain 14 to 18 grams of protein and 85 to 90 calories

- 3 ounces of skinless turkey or chicken breast contain 25 grams of protein and 120 to 150 calories

- 3 ounces of imitation seafood contain 10 grams of protein and 87 calories

Sample Meal Plan

Here's a meal plan that will yield 74 grams of protein, 445 calories, and 56 ounces of fluids:

Begin your day by taking your fluids from 7 to 7:30. In this sample, consume 12 ounces of crystal light. From 8 to 9:00 in the morning, consume your first meal, which is half a cup of egg beaters. Take your fluids, 8 ounces of water, from 9:30 to 11:30. Consume your 2nd meal, 3 ounces of tuna salad with fat-free mayonnaise, from 12 to 1:00.

Take your fluids again, 24 ounces of Power Aid Zero, from 1:30 to 3:00. Consume your third meal, 8 ounces of light yogurt, from 3:30 to 4:00. From 4:30 to 6:00, take your fluids, which is 12 ounces of water. You will consume your 4th meal from 6:30 to 7:30, which is 3 ounces of haddock and 1/4 cup of mashed potatoes. Eat your last meal for the day, 4 ounces of Greek yogurt, from 9:00 to 9:30.

Second Phase Sample Recipe

Steamed Fish with Yogurt Dill Sauce

Here are the needed ingredients for this dish:

- 1/2 cup of reduced-sodium and fat-free chicken broth

- 1 scallion, finely chopped

- 2 tablespoons of extra virgin olive oil

- 1 tablespoon of fresh dill

- 1 teaspoon of finely minced fresh basil

- 1 lemon, thinly sliced

- Salt and pepper to taste

- 1 tablespoon of finely chopped fresh chives

- 1/3 cup of plain low-fat yogurt

- 4 sprigs of fresh dill for garnish

Mix the basil, chives, half of the dill, and oil in a bowl. Rub the mixture on all sides of the fish. Season with salt and pepper. In another bowl, mix the sauce by combining the yogurt with the rest of the dill.

Arrange the scallions at the bottom of a deep-rimmed serving dish. Put the fish and top with the lemon slices. Add the broth. Cook in the microwave at a medium temperature setting until the fish is easily flaked using a fork. Garnish with dill and serve the dish with the prepared sauce.

10 - The Third Period: High Protein, Low-Fat, Low-Sugar Diet

This period starts one month after the procedure. At this stage, you are feeling better and it is easier to eat bread and meat. This doesn't mean that you can go back to your old eating habits. The success of your weight loss plans still depend on your commitment to eating healthy food and staying away from sweets and alcohol.

There are times when you will find eating and drinking more difficult than the earlier weeks. This means that the connection of the small intestine and stomach is healing. A scar is forming at the connection site, which makes it narrower and thicker. As a result, the movement of anything that you drink or eat takes a longer time to pass through the connection.

At this phase, you can incorporate more solid and easily chewable foods. When eating solid food items, reduce the number of meals you have to three per day but do not go any less than that. The interval between meals is 4 to 5 hours. Concentrate on your food while eating. Cut your food into small portions and allow 20 to 30 minutes in eating each meal.

You must still pay attention to the pressure at the back of your sternum, which signifies that your pouch is full and that you must stop eating. Do not overeat. If it happens often, your stomach will stretch and will make the whole process useless.

Your goal is to take in more than 64 ounces of fluids per day. Your protein intake per day is 65 to 90 grams. Every meal must have a protein-rich food, and make it a habit to eat them first. You can stop taking protein drinks only if you are certain that you are getting the necessary amount of protein from what you eat.

Introduce one new food per day. Eat food items that are low-fat and healthy and avoid anything that contains easily absorbed carbohydrates and sweets. Aim for 900-1000 kilocalorie per day from here on until the end of the first year after undergoing the procedure.

Here are the foods that you may find hard to tolerate this stage

- Fruits with hard skin and many seeds

- Red meat

- Hard or cartilaginous meat

- Whole milk

- Apple

- Ice cream

- Fruits with tough skin

- Grapes

- Fruit bread

- Noodles

- Condensed milk

- Nuts

- Chili and spicy foods

- Rice

- Potato peels

- Grain bread with pieces of fruits and nuts

- Chewing gum

- Sweets

To achieve the biggest weight loss, limit or avoid the following food items:

- Fast noodle food

- High-fat cream soups

- Meat products and vegetables, fried and covered with breadcrumbs

- Condensed milk

- Chocolate milk

- Fried eggs

- Donuts

- Danish pastries

- Fast foods

- Sweet bread

- Fried salty snacks

- Fruits with added sugar

- Ice cream

- Whole milk

Liquid Consumption

Like in the previous phases, you have to sip your liquids in a slow manner. The required amount of fluid intake per day is 1.2 to 1.5 liters. Do not drink half an hour before and after eating.

Here's a list of the allowed drinks to take in this phase:

Water

- Non-carbonated flavored water

- Juices diluted in water

- Sugar-free tea

Here are the drinks that you ought to avoid:

- Carbonated drinks

- Soft drinks

- Drinks with sweet sugar

- Sports drinks

Allowed Vitamins and Medicines

Continue taking the following items from the previous phase:

- 1 multivitamin tablet twice a day

- Vitamin B12 replacement therapy with injections

- 30 microgram D3-vitamin tablet once per day

- 600-milligram Calcium nitrate tablets twice a day

- 100-milligram of iron preparations once every other day for women in fertile age

Physical Activity

It is now time to develop a regular exercise routine. Make sure that you walk at least an hour and 30 minutes every day. You are no longer restricted to lift weights. You can now perform challenging exercises to burn calories and build muscles.

Sample Meal Plan

Here's a meal plan that will yield 735 calories, 69 grams of protein, 9 grams of fat, and 94 grams of carbohydrates.

Breakfast starts at 8 to 8:30. In this sample, eat 1/2 slice of toasted dry whole wheat bread and 1 scrambled egg. Take your snacks and fluids from 9 to 11:30, which include 8 ounces of flavored water, 8 ounces of tea, decaffeinated coffee, or water.

Eat the following for lunch scheduled from 12 noon to

12:30: 2 saltine crackers, 1 cup of lentil soup, 1/2 canned peach with no syrup and no sugar added, and 2 baby carrots. From 2:30 to 5:30, take your snacks and fluids, such as 8 ounces of zero-calorie beverage, 6 ounces of fat-free light yogurt, and 12 ounces of water.

Dinner comes at 6 to 6:30 and is composed of 1/4 cup of steamed rice sprayed with diet margarine, 3 ounces of baked haddock with lemon, 1/4 cup of strawberries, and 1/4 of steamed broccoli. Take your snacks and fluids from 7 to 10 in the evening, which include 12 ounces of flavored water, 1/2 fat-free ricotta cheese, and 12 ounces of water.

11 - Bariatric-Friendly Breakfast Recipes

Here are the recipes that you can prepare when you are in your last phase of the healing period and for the rest of your life to maintain the weight you've lost and keep your ideal figure.

Breakfast Pancakes with Peanut Butter and Jelly

This recipe contains 10 grams of protein, 1.5 grams of fat, 9 grams of carbohydrates, and 90 calories per serving size of 1 pancake.

The following ingredients will yield 4 servings of this dish:

- 4 egg whites

- 2 tablespoons of powdered peanuts

- 1/2 cup of instant oatmeal

- 1/2 cup of low-fat cottage cheese

- 1 cup of frozen mixed berry blend

Process the following ingredients in a blender: cottage cheese, oatmeal, peanuts, and egg whites. Stop the blender once it looks like a pancake batter. Transfer the mixture to a bowl. Fold in the berry fruit mix and cook the pancakes in a greased skillet.

Pumpkin Pie Oatmeal

This recipe contains 14 grams of protein, 3 grams of fat, 34 grams of carbohydrates, and 205 calories per serving.

Here are the needed ingredients to make a serving of this dish:

- 1/2 cup of 1 percent cottage cheese with no salt added

- 1/2 cup of canned pumpkin

- 30 grams of old-fashioned oats

- 1/8 teaspoon of cinnamon

- 1 teaspoon of Truvia baking blend

- A dash each of ground cloves and ground ginger

Put the oats in a heatproof bowl. Add the pumpkin, sweetener, and spices. Mix well. Cook in the microwave on a high setting for 90 seconds. Stir in the cottage cheese. Put back in the microwave and cook for 60 seconds. Leave at a room temperature for a couple of minutes before serving.

Yogurt Popsicles

This recipe contains 5 grams of protein, 0.6 gram of fat, 11 grams of carbohydrates, and 75 calories per serving size of 1 popsicle.

Prepare the following ingredients to make 6 popsicles:

- 1/2 cup of skim milk or 1 percent milk

- 1 cup of non-fat and plain Greek yogurt

- 1/2 cup or instant or regular oats

- 1 cup of chopped fruits or mixed berries

Mix milk and yogurt in a bowl until combined. Transfer it into 6 popsicle molds. Divide the berries and oats into each mold. Put in the freezer for a minute. Insert popsicle sticks into the molds. Put back into the freezer until set and firm.

Tuna Sandwiches with Apple

This recipe contains 23 grams of protein, 2.5 grams of fat, 30 grams of carbohydrates, and 250 calories per serving size of 1/3 of the recipe.

Get the following ingredients ready to make 3 sandwiches:

- 3 lettuce leaves, rinsed

- 1 6.5-ounce can of tuna, drained

- 1/2 teaspoon of honey

- 1/4 cup of low-fat vanilla yogurt

- 6 slices of whole wheat bread

- 1 apple, peeled, washed, and cut into small pieces

- 1 teaspoon of mustard

Mix the yogurt, apple, mustard, honey, and tuna in a bowl. Lay 3 bread slices and spread them with half of the mixture. Put a lettuce leaf and the other slice of each bread on top of each sandwich.

High-Protein Cottage Cheese Pancakes

This recipe contains 13 grams of protein, 7 grams of fat, 10 grams of carbohydrates, and 152 calories per serving size of 1 pancake.

Here are the necessary ingredients to make 3 servings of the dish:

- 1/3 cup of all-purpose flour

- 1 cup of low-fat cottage cheese

- 1/2 teaspoon of baking soda

- 1/2 tablespoon of canola oil

- 3 eggs, lightly beaten

Mix the flour and baking soda in a bowl. Put the remaining ingredients in another bowl and mix until combined. Gradually combine the two mixtures. Cook 1/3 of the batter at a time in a greased skillet over medium heat. Top the pancakes with low-calorie syrup before serving.

Protein Loaded Pumpkin-Ricotta Pie

This recipe contains 6 grams of protein, 3.5 grams of fat, 10 grams of carbohydrates, and 105 calories per serving size of 1 slice.

Here are the necessary ingredients to make 12 servings of the dish:

- 2-ounce pack of pecan halves

- 1 cup of nonfat milk

- 2 eggs

- 1 teaspoon each of ground nutmeg and ground cinnamon

- 2 scoops of Whey Protein Isolate (100% unflavored)

- 1/2 teaspoon of salt

- 1/3 cup of Splenda Sugar Blend

- 1 cup of part skim ricotta cheese

- 2 cups of 100 percent pure canned pumpkin puree with no added salt

Put the ricotta cheese, 1/2 cup of milk, and eggs in a blender. Process until smooth. Put the remaining ingredients and process until blended. Transfer the batter to a greased pie dish. Put the pecans on top. Bake for 45 minutes in a preheated oven at 350 degrees. Transfer to a wire rack and leave for an hour to cool. Slice into 12 and serve.

Hot and Spicy Deviled Eggs

This recipe contains 10 grams of protein, 8.7 grams of fat, 1 gram of carbohydrates, and 131 calories per serving size of 2 deviled eggs.

Prepare the following ingredients to make 3 servings of this dish:

- 1/2 teaspoon of dill

- 6 hard-boiled eggs, peeled

- A dash of paprika and black pepper

- 1/8 teaspoon of salt

- 2 tablespoons of Greek yogurt

- 1/4 teaspoon of spicy mustard

Cut the eggs in half. Scoop out the egg yolks. Put the 3 cooked yolks in a bowl and keep the other 3 in the fridge and use for another recipe. Mix the 3 egg yolks and yogurt. Gradually mash while adding the mustard, dill, and salt. Divide the mixture to fill each half of the egg white. Season with pepper and paprika before serving.

Breakfast Egg-Chilada

This recipe contains 23 grams of protein, 8 grams of fat, 3 grams of carbohydrates, and 171 calories per serving size of 1 egg-chilada.

Here are the needed ingredients to make a serving of this dish:

- 2 tablespoons of salsa

- 1 ounce chicken, tofu, or ground beef

- Salt and black pepper to taste

- 1 egg, plus 1 egg white, beaten

- 1 tablespoon of shredded Mexican blend cheese

- 2 tablespoons of plain and fat-free Greek yogurt

Spread the beaten eggs in a greased skillet over medium heat. Allow to set for 2 minutes before sprinkling with salt and pepper. Flip the eggs and cook the other side for a couple of minutes.

Transfer to a plate. In a bowl, combine the protein of choice, chicken, tofu, or ground beef, and cheese. Turn the mixture into a strip and put on top of the egg pancake. Roll the pancake to wrap the filling. Top with salsa and yogurt before serving.

Egg Muffin

This recipe contains 8 grams of protein, 7 grams of fat, 1 gram of carbohydrates, and 98 calories per serving size of 1 muffin.

The following ingredients will yield 12 servings of this dish:

- 12 slices of turkey bacon, cooked and sliced into

thirds

- 1/2 cup of 1 percent milk

- 6 eggs

- 3/4 cup of shredded low-fat Swiss cheese

- 1/4 teaspoon each of Italian seasoning, salt, and pepper

Grease 12 muffin cups. Put 3 bacon slices in each cup. Set aside 1/4 cup of cheese. Put the remaining ingredients in a bowl and mix well. Scoop out 1/4 of the mixture on top of the bacon slices. Sprinkle cheese on top. Bake for 25 minutes in a preheated oven at 350 degrees.

Berry Breakfast Wrap

This recipe contains 8 grams of protein, 9 grams of fat, 30 grams of carbohydrates, and 233 calories per serving size of 1 tortilla wrap.

You will need the following ingredients to make a serving of this dish:

- 1 tablespoon of low-sugar strawberry jelly

- 3 tablespoons of regular ricotta cheese

- 1 tortilla (whole wheat)

- 1/3 cup of sliced fresh strawberries

Lay the tortilla on a plate. Spread it with cheese and jelly. Add the berries on top. Roll the tortilla to wrap the filling.

Quinoa Bowl with Tofu

This recipe contains 12 grams of protein, 10 grams of fat, 27 grams of carbohydrates, and 232 calories per serving size of 1/6 of the recipe.

To make 6 servings of this dish, you will need the following:

- 2/3 cup of chopped scallions

- 1 15-ounce pack of extra firm tofu, diced

- 1 cup of shredded carrots

- 1 cup of uncooked quinoa

- 1 tablespoon of sesame oil

- 2 tablespoons of soy sauce

- 1/2 cup each of fresh cilantro and toasted slivered almonds

- 1 1/2 cups of chicken broth

For the sauce, you will need:

Juice of 1/2 lime

- 1 teaspoon of grated ginger

- 1 garlic clove, minced

- 2 tablespoons each of rice wine vinegar and Sriracha sauce

- 1/2 tablespoon of brown sugar

- 3 tablespoons of coconut milk

- 2 teaspoons of creamy peanut butter

Rinse the tofu and drain the liquid 30 minutes before cooking. Transfer them to a plate lined with a dish towel. Place another plate on top. This will provide the weight to get rid of the excess liquid.

Leave for half an hour. Put the sesame oil, tofu, and soy sauce in a bowl. Toss to combine. Transfer to a baking sheet and bake for 40 minutes. Toss the ingredients every 10 minutes and continue baking until all sides are crisp.

Toast the quinoa in a saucepan over medium-low flame for 5 minutes while constantly stirring. Turn the heat to low and add the broth. Cover the pan and simmer for 15 minutes. Fluff the cooked quinoa using a fork.

Mix the sauce in a heatproof bowl. Put the peanut butter and microwave for 10 seconds or until melted. Stir in the remaining ingredients and whisk to combine. Put the veggies, toasted almonds, herbs, tofu, and quinoa in a bowl. Add the sauce and mix well.

Crustless Quiche with Cheese

This recipe contains 19.5 grams of protein, 9 grams of fat, 3.6 grams of carbohydrates, and 176 calories per serving size of 1/8 of the recipe.

Here are the necessary ingredients to make 8 servings of the dish:

- 1 cup of skim milk

- 6 ounces of chicken breast, cut into cubes and grilled

- 3 eggs

- Non-stick cooking spray

- 4 ounces of low-fat Baby Swiss, cut into cubes

- Oregano as seasoning

- 10 ounces of shredded low-fat mozzarella cheese

Lay the baby Swiss and chicken breast in a pie pan. Add the shredded mozzarella cheese on top and sprinkle with oregano. Whisk the eggs and skim milk in a bowl. Pour this on top of the pan. Bake for 40 minutes in a preheated oven at 400 degrees. Leave to cool before serving.

12 - Bariatric-Friendly Seafood and Vegetables Recipes

Healthy Tuna Patty

This recipe contains 12 grams of protein, 1 gram of fat, 4 grams of carbohydrates, and 80 calories per serving size of 1/8 of the recipe.

To make 8 servings of the dish, you will need the following ingredients:

- 1 tablespoon of chopped onion

- 4 egg whites

- 16 crushed crackers

- 1/4 cup each of diced red pepper, capers, and chopped water chestnuts

- 4 3-ounce cans of tuna in water

- Dill, pepper, and dried mustard to taste

The first step is to put all the ingredients in a bowl. Mix well. Divide them into 8 and shape each into a patty. Cook the patties in a greased skillet over medium heat until both sides are browned.

You can opt to serve this along with 1 spoon of fat-free Greek yogurt.

Broiled Orange Roughy

This recipe contains 17 grams of protein, 4 grams of fat, 3 grams of carbohydrates, and 114 calories per serving size of 1 cup.

Here are the ingredients that you will need to make 4 servings of this dish:

- 1 tablespoon each of Dijon mustard and olive oil

- 8 lemon wedges

- 3 tablespoons of lemon juice

- 1/4 teaspoon of ground pepper

- 16 ounces of orange roughy fillets

Combine the lemon juice, ground pepper, olive oil, and

mustard in a bowl. Pu the fillets on a baking sheet that is lined with greased foil. Brush the fish with half of the lemon juice. Broil for 5 minutes. Drizzle the rest of the lemon juice on top of the broiled fillets. Top with the lemon wedges and season with pepper before serving.

Cheesy Broccoli with Egg

This recipe contains 12 grams of protein, 5 grams of fat, 5 grams of carbohydrates, and 115 calories per serving size of 1 slice.

The following ingredients are needed to make 8 servings of the dish:

- 6 eggs

- 1/2 cup of sliced mushrooms

- 10 ounces of chopped broccoli

- 1 teaspoon of salt

- 1/2 pound of low-fat cheddar cheese

- 6 tablespoons of flour

- 2 pounds of nonfat cottage cheese

- 1 4-ounce jar of chopped pimento

- A dash each of black pepper and paprika

This is easy to do. Simply mix all the ingredients in a bowl. Transfer the mixture to a greased pan. Bake for 90 minutes in a preheated oven at 350 degrees.

This is best eaten while hot.

Vegetarian Pizza with Ranch Dressing

This recipe contains 10 grams of protein, 10 grams of fat, 12 grams of carbohydrates, and 170 calories per serving size of 1/4 tortilla.

Prepare the following ingredients to make 4 servings of this healthy snack:

- 1/8 cup of shredded carrots

- 1 pack of dry mix ranch dressing

- 1/2 cup of low-fat chive and onion cream cheese

- 1/2 cup of light sour cream

- 3/4 cup each of shredded Colby & Monterey Jack cheese, diced tomatoes, and raw broccoli

- 2 large low-carb tortilla wraps

- 1/8 cup each of diced green pepper and diced cucumber

Put the packet of ranch dressing in a bowl. Mix it with cream cheese and sour cream. Lay the tortillas and spread them with the mixture. Add the vegetables and olives on top, plus a generous heap of cheese. Slice each to tortilla into 4 before serving.

Pureed Cauliflower

This recipe contains 5 grams of protein, 6 grams of fat, 13 grams of carbohydrates, and 113 calories per serving size of 3/4 cup.

To make 4 serving of the dish, you will need the following:

- 1/3 cup of low-fat buttermilk

- 1 teaspoon of salted butter

- 3 garlic cloves

- 4 teaspoons of extra-virgin olive oil

- 1/2 teaspoon each of garlic salt and black pepper

- 1 large cauliflower head

First, steam the cauliflower head along with the garlic cloves. Chop the cauliflower into small pieces and put them in a heatproof bowl. Add the garlic cloves and 1/4 cup of water. Cover the bowl before putting it inside the microwave oven. Steam in the microwave for 5 minutes on a high setting.

Put the steamed garlic cloves in the food processor and process until crushed. Add the buttermilk, steamed cauliflower, pepper, 2 teaspoons of olive oil, butter, and garlic salt. Process until the mixture looks creamy.

Transfer to a serving bowl and drizzle with the remaining

olive oil before serving.

French Toast with Stuffing

This recipe contains 25 grams of protein, 0.5 gram of fat, 27 grams of carbohydrates, and 227 calories per serving.

The following ingredients will yield a serving of this recipe:

- 4 slices of low-calorie bread

- 3 egg whites

- 1/4 teaspoon of pumpkin pie spice

- 2 packets of sugar substitute

- A dash each of salt and vanilla

- 1/2 cup of fat-free ricotta cheese

Lay 2 slices of bread and spread them with ricotta cheese. Sprinkle them with the sugar substitute. Cover each slice with the remaining bread slices.

Whisk the egg whites on a bowl. Add salt, vanilla, and 1/4

teaspoon of pumpkin pie spice. Mix well. Dip the sandwiches into the mixture. Fry them in a greased skillet over medium heat until both sides are browned.

Vegetarian Chili with Cheese

This recipe contains 13 grams of protein, 3 grams of fat, 34 grams of carbohydrates, and 195 calories per serving size of 1 1/2 cups.

To make 8 servings of this dish, you will need the following:

- 8 ounces of tomato sauce

- 1 14.5-ounce can of diced tomatoes

- 1 zucchini (sliced)

- 2 garlic cloves

- 1/2 pound of mushrooms (sliced)

- 2 tablespoons of chili powder

- 1 10-ounce pack of frozen corn

- 2 15-ounce cans of red kidney beans (rinsed and drained)

- 1 green bell pepper (chopped)

- 1 cup of chopped onion

- 2 teaspoons of olive oil

- 1 cup of shredded low-fat cheddar cheese

Heat pan over medium-high flame. Add oil. Put the garlic once the oil is heated and sauté for a couple of minutes. Stir in the onions, pepper, and mushrooms, and cook for 3 minutes. Add the tomato sauce, diced tomatoes, and chili powder. Simmer for 15 minutes. Stir in the fresh corn and half a cup of the cheese. Simmer for 15 more minutes. Sprinkle cheddar cheese on top before serving.

Broccoli Quiche with Tofu

This recipe contains 13 grams of protein, 8 grams of fat, 18 grams of carbohydrates, and 190 calories per serving size of 1/6 of the recipe.

Here are the ingredients that you will need to make 6 servings of the dish:

- 1 yellow onion (sliced)

- 1 1/2 pounds of tofu

- A pinch of salt

- 2 tablespoons of sesame tahini

- 1/2 cup of uncooked bulgur wheat

- 1/2 pound of broccoli (chopped)

- 1 tablespoon each of sesame oil, white miso, and tamari

- 1/4 pound of mushrooms (chopped)

Put 1 cup of water in a pot over medium-high heat. Once it boils, add salt and the bulgur. Bring to another boil. Lower the heat and cover the pot. Simmer for 15 minutes. Put the cooked bulgur into an oiled pie pan. Press to make it firm. Bake for 12 minutes in a preheated oven at 350 degrees. Set this aside.

Heat oil in a skillet over medium-high flame. Put the onions, broccoli, and mushrooms. Sauté for 2 minutes. Cover the skillet and remove from heat. Set this aside.

Put the tamari, white miso, tofu, and tahini in a food processor. Process until smooth.

Transfer the cooked vegetables in a bowl. Add the tofu mixture and toss to combine. Transfer them to the bulgur crust. Bake for 30 minutes. Allow to cool for 10 minutes before slicing into 6 pieces.

Ratatouille

This recipe contains 4.5 grams of protein, 2 grams of fat, 9 grams of carbohydrates, and 335 calories per serving.

The following ingredients will yield 4 servings of this healthy recipe:

- 1 red capsicum (diced)

- 2 zucchinis (diced)

- 1 onion (chopped)

- 1 garlic clove (crushed)

- 1 eggplant (diced)

- 1 stick of celery (diced)

- 400 grams of tomatoes (chopped and with no added salt)

- Oil spray

- 1/4 cup of fresh basil (chopped)

- 2 cups of mushrooms (diced)

Lightly grease a pan over medium heat. Cook the onion and garlic for a couple of minutes. Add the celery, mushrooms, and capsicum, and sauté for 4 minutes. Transfer to a plate and set aside.

Spray the same pan with a bit of oil. Cook the zucchinis and eggplant until soft. Stir in the basil and basil, and put back the mushroom mixture. Lower the heat and simmer for 5 minutes.

Freeze any leftover and reheat when needed.

Shrimp Ceviche

This recipe contains 25 grams of protein, 1 gram of fat, 13 grams of carbohydrates, and 160 calories per serving size of 4 ounces.

Here are the needed ingredients to make 4 servings of this dish:

- 2 serrano chili peppers (minced)

- 3/4 cup of red onion (chopped)

- 1 pound of raw shrimp

- 1 cup of lime juice

- 1 bunch of cilantro (chopped)

- 4 tomatoes (diced)

Put the shrimp in a bowl. Drizzle with lime juice. Make sure that all the pieces of shrimp are covered with the juice. Cover the bowl and leave for 15 minutes to marinate.

Take note of the time. Do not marinate the shrimp for more than 15 minutes because they will become tough. Add the onions, tomatoes, cilantro, and chili peppers, and mix well until combined. Season with salt and pepper before serving.

Black Bean with Pumpkin Soup

This recipe contains 15 grams of protein, 6 grams of fat, 46 grams of carbohydrates, and 290 calories per serving size of 1 cup.

You will need the following ingredients to make 6 servings of this dish:

- 1 16-ounce can of pumpkin puree

- 2 15-ounce cans of black beans (rinsed and drained)

- 1 cup of diced tomatoes (canned)

- 2 cups of beef broth

- 4 garlic cloves (chopped)

- 1/2 teaspoon of black pepper

- 2 tablespoons of olive oil

- 1 tablespoon of ground cumin

- 1 teaspoon of chili powder

- 1 onion (chopped)

Put oil in a pan over medium heat. Cook the onion and garlic for a couple of minutes. Season with the cumin, chili powder, and pepper. Stir in the tomatoes, black beans, and pumpkin. Add the broth. Simmer for 25 minutes while occasionally stirring. You can serve the soup as is or puree using an immersion blender.

Black Bean and Corn Salad

This recipe contains 6 grams of protein, 5 grams of fat, 23 grams of carbohydrates, and 160 calories per serving size of 1/2 cup.

Prepare the following ingredients to make 6 servings of this dish:

- 1/4 teaspoon of ground black pepper

- 2 16-ounce cans of black beans, rinsed and drained

- 2 tablespoons each of olive oil and minced red onion

- 1 cup of whole kernel corn

- A dash of salt

- 1 teaspoon each of minced garlic, lemon juice and brown sugar

- 1/4 cup each of balsamic vinegar and chopped fresh parsley

Put the fresh corn, black beans, red onion, and fresh parsley in a bowl and mix. In another bowl, mix the honey, garlic, balsamic vinegar, olive oil, salt and pepper, and lemon juice. Mix until combined. Combine the 2 mixtures. Leave for 30 minutes before serving.

Spicy Peanut Vegetarian Chili

This recipe contains 8 grams of protein, 2.5 grams of fat, 22 grams of carbohydrates, and 125 calories per serving size of 1/2 cup.

Here are the needed ingredients to make 12 servings of this dish:

- 2 tablespoons of chili powder

- 1 28-ounce can of diced tomato

- 1 16-ounce can each of white beans and white beans, rinsed and drained

- 1 cup of chopped onion

- 1 15-ounce can of tomato sauce

- 2 garlic cloves, minced

- 2 cups of vegetable broth

- 1/4 teaspoon of dried oregano

- 1 tablespoon of peanut oil

- 1 teaspoon of chipotle chili pepper

- 1/3 cup of powdered peanuts

Heat oil in a pot over medium-high flame. Add the onion and garlic. Cook for 4 minutes. Stir in the chili powder, salt, pepper, and oregano. Sauté for 2 minutes. Add the beans, tomato sauce, corn, tomatoes, powdered peanuts, and broth. Stir the ingredients. Bring it to a boil. Turn the heat to low and leave for 30 minutes to simmer.

13 - Bariatric-Friendly Meat Recipes

Chicken with Peanut and Applesauce

This recipe contains 3 grams of protein, 2 grams of fat, 13 grams of carbohydrates, and 50 calories per serving size of 2 tablespoons.

The following ingredients will yield 8 servings of this dish:

- 2 1/2 pounds of sliced chicken

- 1/4 cup of yellow mustard

- 1 15-ounce jar of unsweetened applesauce

- Salt and pepper to taste

- 1/8 cup of unpacked Splenda brown sugar

- 1/2 cup of powdered peanuts

Heat pan over medium-high flame. Put the meat and saute for a couple of minutes. Add the brown sugar, peanuts, mustard, and applesauce. Stir the ingredients until combined. Reduce the heat to medium. Simmer for 10 minutes.

Chicken Cheesesteak Wrap

This recipe contains 33 grams of protein, 6 grams of fat, 17 grams of carbohydrates, and 264 calories per serving size of 1 wrap.

You will need the following ingredients to make a serving of this dish:

- 1 whole wheat low-carb tortilla

- 1/4 pound of skinless and boneless chicken breast, with the visible fat trimmed and thinly sliced into strips

- 1 3/4-ounce wedge of light Swiss cheese

- 1/4 cup each of chopped onions, sliced green pepper, and sliced mushrooms

- 2 teaspoons of sliced pickled hot chili peppers

Heat oil in a skillet over medium flame. Cook the onion and meat until done. Stir in the green peppers and mushroom. Cook for 4 minutes. Lay the tortilla in the middle of 2 moist paper towels. Microwave for 20 seconds on a high setting. Add a strip of cheese in the middle. Put the chicken, onions, peppers, mushrooms, and onions on top. Add chili peppers if you want it to be spicier. Fold the tortilla before serving.

Chicken Taco Filling

This recipe contains 23 grams of protein, 2.4 grams of fat, 6 grams of carbohydrates, and 148 calories per serving size of 4 ounces.

To make 4 servings of this dish, you will need the following:

- 1 pound of skinless and boneless chicken breasts

- 1 cup of chicken broth

- 1 1.25-ounce pack of dry taco seasoning mix

Put the chicken broth in a bowl and mix it with the taco seasoning. Place the meat in a slow cooker. Pour the seasoning mixture over the meat. Lock the lid in place and cook for 8 hours. Shred the chicken and continue cooking for 30 minutes.

Use the cooked mixture as filling for tacos or as toppings for salads.

Baked Chicken and Veggies

This recipe contains 26 grams of protein, 3.5 grams of fat, 25 grams of carbohydrates, and 240 calories per serving size of 1/6 of the recipe.

Here are the necessary ingredients to make 6 servings of the dish:

- 1 raw chicken, skinless and cut into bite-size pieces

- 6 carrots, sliced

- 1 teaspoon of thyme

- 4 potatoes, sliced

- 1/2 cup of water

- 1 onion, quartered

- 1/4 teaspoon of pepper

Lay the potatoes, onions, and carrots at the bottom of a large roasting pan. Place the meat on top. In a bowl, mix water, pepper, and thyme. Add the mixture to the pan. Bake in a preheated oven at 400 degrees for 1 hour. Twice during the process, get the pan from the oven and spoon over the juices on top. Bake until the meat is tender.

Chicken Caprese

This recipe contains 33 grams of protein, 9 grams of fat, 4 grams of carbohydrates, and 230 calories per serving size of 1 ounce each of cheese and tomato, and 4 ounces of chicken.

Prepare the following ingredients to make 4 servings of this dish:

- 3 tablespoons of balsamic vinegar

- 1 pound of skinless and boneless chicken breasts

- 1 tablespoon of olive oil

- 1 ripe tomato, quartered

- Pepper, to taste

- 2 tablespoons of thinly sliced basil

- 4 slices of fresh mozzarella cheese

- 1 teaspoon of dry Italian seasoning

Put the meat in a bowl and season with oil, pepper, and dry Italian seasoning. Put the seasoned meat on a preheated grill over medium-high heat. Grill each side for 5 minutes or until well-done. Sprinkle the mozzarella cheese on top. Cook for 1 more minute before transferring to a plate. Top each piece of meat with pepper, basil, 1 slice of tomato and balsamic vinegar before serving.

Creamy Chicken in Slow Cooker

This recipe contains 18.5 grams of protein, 1.68 grams of fat, and 128 calories per serving size of 6 ounces.

Here are the necessary ingredients to make 6 servings of the dish:

- 1/2 cup of chicken stock

- 1 cup of plain Greek yogurt

- 1 8-ounce pack of mushrooms

- 2.5 pounds of skinless and boneless chicken breasts

- 1 7-ounce envelope of Italian dressing mix

- 1 10-ounce can of low-fat cream of mushroom soup

Heat a greased skillet over medium-high flame. Cook the meat in batches until browned. Put the browned meat in a slow cooker. Pour the soup into the same skillet. Add the Italian dressing mix, chicken stock, and yogurt.

Stir the mixture until combined. Pour the soup over the meat in the slow cooker. Add the mushrooms. Lock the lid in place and cook for 4 hours on low setting. Stir the soup before serving.

Brown Rice and Beans Casserole

This recipe contains 31 grams of protein, 6 grams of fat, 22 grams of carbohydrates, and 267 calories per serving size of 1/8 of the recipe.

Prepare the following ingredients to make 8 servings of this dish:

- 1 4-ounce can of green chilies, diced

- 16 ounces of skinless and boneless chicken breasts, chopped

- 1/2 teaspoon of cumin

- 1 cup of vegetable broth

- 1 tablespoon of olive oil

- 1/3 cup each of brown rice and diced onion

- 1 zucchini, sliced

- 1 15-ounce can of black beans, drained

- 1/3 cup of shredded carrots

- 2 cups shredded low-fat Swiss cheese

- 1/4 teaspoon of cayenne pepper

- 1/2 cup of sliced mushrooms

Mix the rice and broth in a pot over medium-high flame. Bring to a boil. Cover the pot and reduce the heat to low. Simmer for 45 minutes or until the rice is tender. Heat oil in a skillet over medium flame. Put the onion and sauté for 3 minutes. Stir in the zucchini, seasonings, mushrooms, and meat. Cook for 5 minutes.

Transfer the cooked rice to a bowl. Pour over the cooked meat and zucchini mixture. Add the chilies, carrots, beans, and 1 cup of Swiss cheese. Mix thoroughly until combined. Transfer the mixture to an oiled casserole dish.

Sprinkle the remaining cheese on top. Cover the casserole dish with loose foil. Bake for half an hour in a preheated oven at 350 degrees. Remove the foil and continue baking for 10 more minutes.

Chicken with Greek Yogurt

This recipe contains 46 grams of protein, 4 grams of fat, 3 grams of carbohydrates, and 266 calories per serving size of 1 cup.

Here are the needed ingredients to make 4 servings of this dish:

- 4 skinless and boneless chicken breasts

- 1 cup of plain Greek yogurt

- 1/2 cup of grated Parmesan cheese

- 1 1/2 teaspoons of salt

- 1 teaspoon of garlic powder

- 1/2 teaspoon of pepper

Mix the Greek yogurt, seasonings, and cheese in a bowl. Season the meat with the mixture. Arrange the coated meat on a greased baking sheet lined with foil. Bake for 45 minutes in a preheated oven at 375 degrees.

Southwest Pasta Salad with Chicken

This recipe contains 21 grams of protein, 9.9 grams of fat, 38.2 grams of carbohydrates, and 322 calories per serving size of 1 1/3 cups.

The following ingredients will yield 6 servings of this dish:

- 1/2 pound of uncooked penne rigate

- 1 cup of fresh corn kernels

- 2 cups of skinless and boneless lemon-herb chicken,

grilled

- 1 tablespoon each of extra-virgin olive oil and canned chipotle chili in adobo, chopped

- 1/2 teaspoon of salt

- 2 tablespoons of fresh lime juice

- 1/2 cup each of diced red bell pepper, chopped plum tomato, and sliced green onions

- 1/4 cup of fresh orange juice

- 3 ounces of shredded sharp cheddar cheese

Remove the fat and salt from the package of the penne rigate and cook according to instructions. Drain the liquid. Put the cooked pasta in a bowl. Add the corn kernels, red bell pepper, meat, cheese, green onions, and tomato.

Toss the ingredients until combined. Mix all the remaining ingredients in another bowl. Pour this over the pasta mixture and gently toss. Cover the bowl and leave in the fridge for at least 30 minutes before serving.

Faux Fried Chicken

This recipe contains 29 grams of protein, 3.5 grams of fat, 17 grams of carbohydrates, and 210 calories per serving size of 3 pieces.

You will need the following ingredients to make 3 servings of this dish:

- 1/3 cup each of panko breadcrumbs, bran cereal, and reduced-fat buttermilk

- 12 ounces of skinless and boneless lean chicken breasts

- Salt to taste

- 1 tablespoon of dry onion soup mix

- 1/8 teaspoon of paprika

Mix the buttermilk and paprika in a bag. Put the meat. Seal the bag and shake until all sides of the meat is coated with the mixture. Refrigerate for 1 hour. Process the cereal in the food processor until it has the same consistency as breadcrumbs. Transfer to a bowl.

Add the panko breadcrumbs and onion soup. Mix until combined. Season with salt. Coat the meat with the mixture and arrange all pieces on an oiled baking sheet. Bake for 10 minutes in a preheated oven at 375 degrees. Flip the meat and continue baking for 10 more minutes.

Super Moist Chicken

This recipe contains 37 grams of protein, 5 grams of fat, 8 grams of carbohydrates, and 233 calories per serving size of 1 cup.

To make 12 servings of this dish, you will need the following:

- 1 1/4 cups of whole wheat Italian bread crumbs

- 1/2 cup of light mayo of choice

- 3 pounds of skinless and boneless chicken breasts

Brush all sides of the meat with light mayo. Roll the coated meat in bread crumbs and arrange them in a pan lined with foil. Bake for 45 minutes in a preheated oven at 425 degrees.

Chicken Casserole

This recipe contains 19 grams of protein, 8 grams of fat, 27 grams of carbohydrates, and 256 calories per serving size of 1 cup.

Here are the necessary ingredients to make 4 servings of the dish:

- 2 cups of frozen mixed vegetables

- 1 cup of skinless and boneless chicken breast, cooked

- 1 cup of 2 percent milk

- 4 ounces of canned mushrooms

- 1 cup of shredded cheddar cheese

- 1/2 cup of uncooked whole wheat pasta

- 3/4 cup of water

- Pepper, onion powder, and garlic powder to taste

- 1 10.5-ounce can of fat-free cream of chicken soup

Cook the pasta and veggies according to package directions. Transfer them to a bowl. Add the chicken, mushrooms, water, soup, 1/2 cup of cheese, and milk. Season with garlic powder, pepper, and onion powder. Stir until mixed. Transfer to a greased casserole dish. Add the rest of the cheese on top. Bake for 30 minutes in a preheated oven at 350 degrees.

Chicken Tetrazzini

This recipe contains 10 grams of protein, 3 grams of fat, 25 grams of carbohydrates, and 167 calories per serving size of 1 cup.

Prepare the following ingredients to make 6 servings of this dish:

- 1 cup of fat-free chicken broth

- 1/2 pound of skinless and boneless chicken breasts, cooked and cut into cubes

- 1/2 cup of chopped scallions

- 3 tablespoons of all-purpose flour

- 8 ounces of sliced button mushrooms

- 8 ounces of spaghetti, split into thirds and cooked

- 1/2 cup of fat-free skim milk

- 1 tablespoon of low-calorie margarine

- 2 tablespoons of sherry cooking wine

- 1/4 cup of pimentos, drained and chopped

- 1/4 teaspoon of garlic powder

- 1/8 teaspoon of black pepper

- 3 1/2 tablespoons of grated Parmesan cheese

Melt the margarine in a pan over medium-high heat. Add the scallions and mushrooms. Saute for 5 minutes while stirring frequently. In a bowl, combine the flour, garlic powder, broth, milk, and pepper.

Add this to the pan and cook until it boils. Keep on stirring the mixture until thick. Add the chicken, pimientos, and sherry. Cook for 2 more minutes while occasionally stirring. Add the cheese and cooked spaghetti. Toss the ingredients until combined.

Black Bean Verde and Pork Stew

This recipe contains 33 grams of protein, 7 grams of fat, 25 grams of carbohydrates, and 308 calories per serving size of 1/4 of the recipe.

Here are the needed ingredients to make 4 servings of this dish:

- 3 garlic cloves

- 1 teaspoon each of ground cumin and crushed red pepper flakes

- 1 pound of pork tenderloin, trim the visible fat and cut into cubes

- 2 teaspoons of extra-virgin olive oil

- 1 seasoning packet

- 2 chipotle peppers canned in adobo sauce, minced,

plus 1 teaspoon of the sauce

- 1 1/4 cups of chopped onions

- 1 14.5-ounce of diced tomatoes with no salt added

- 1 14.5-ounce of black beans with no added salt, rinsed and drained

- 1 14-ounce can of chicken broth with no salt added

Put olive oil in a pot over medium-high heat. Once the oil is heated, add the meat and cook until all sides are browned. Stir in the onion and garlic. Cook for 3 more minutes. Add the cumin, chipotle sauce, sauce, and seasoning packet. Mix well. Stir in the tomatoes, beans, red pepper flakes, and broth. Bring to a boil. Reduce the heat to low and cover the pot. Continue cooking for 1 hour.

You can eat the soup as is or pour it over brown rice. Adjust the nutritional content of the dish if you will opt for the latter.

Sweet and Sour Pork Recipe

This recipe contains 18 grams of protein, 3.5 grams of fat,

348 grams of carbohydrates, and 248 calories per serving size of 1/2 cup of rice and 1 cup of the meat mixture.

The following ingredients will yield 6 servings of this dish:

- 3 cups of cooked brown rice

- 2 green peppers, chopped

- 1 15-ounce can of unsweetened pineapple chunks, drained and the juice reserved

- 1 pound of lean pork tenderloin, sliced into thin strips

- 1 onion, chopped

- 2 tablespoons of cornstarch

- 1/4 cup of Splenda brown sugar blend

- 1 tablespoon of low-sodium soy sauce

- 1/2 cup of water

- 1/3 cup of wine vinegar

- 1/2 teaspoon of salt

Heat a greased skillet over medium-high flame. Put the meat and cook until browned. Transfer to a plate and set aside. In a bowl, mix the vinegar, sugar, soy sauce, salt, water, reserved pineapple juice, and cornstarch. Remove the oil from the same skillet and add the mixture.

Cook for 2 minutes while stirring constantly. Put the meat back to the skillet. Reduce the heat to low. Cook for half an hour while stirring every now and then. Stir in the peppers, onion, and pineapple chunks. Cook for 5 minutes. Pour the dish over cooked brown rice and serve.

Asian Pork Tenderloin

This recipe contains 10 grams of protein, 9 grams of fat, 9 grams of carbohydrates, and 256 calories per serving size of 4 ounces.

You will need the following ingredients to make 8 servings of this dish:

- 4 garlic cloves, minced

- 1 1/2 teaspoons of pepper

- 2 pounds of pork tenderloin

- 2 tablespoons each of Worcestershire sauce, lemon juice, dry mustard, and rice vinegar

- 1/3 cup each of brown sugar and light soy sauce

- 1 tablespoon each of ginger and dry mustard

Combine all the ingredients, except the meat, in a freezer bag. Shake well before adding the meat. Seal the bag. Put in the fridge overnight to marinate. The next day, cook the marinated meat in a slow cooker for 6 hours. You can also opt to bake it instead for 40 minutes in a preheated oven at 375 degrees.

Whopper Veggie Burger

This recipe contains 18 grams of protein, 5.5 grams of fat, 40 grams of carbohydrates, and 260 calories per serving size.

To make a serving of this dish, you will need the following:

Onion, Lettuce, and Tomato

- 1 whole wheat hamburger bun

- 1 tablespoon each of ketchup, mustard, and light miracle whip

- 1 savory mushroom mozzarella-flavored Boca Burger

Cook the Boca Burger according to package directions. Use this as filling of a bun. Lay the other ingredients on top, such as the onion, lettuce, ketchup, tomato, and light miracle whip. If you have more time in your hands, you can whip up your own burger by using lean ground turkey breast or ground beef.

Ginger Beef Stir Fry Recipe

This recipe contains 17 grams of protein, 8 grams of fat, 25 grams of carbohydrates, and 275 calories per serving size of 1/6 of the recipe.

Here are the necessary ingredients to make 6 servings of the dish:

- 6 ounces of fat-free beef broth

- 1 pound of flank steak, sliced

- 2 garlic cloves

- 1 teaspoon of canola oil

- 1 8-ounce can of water chestnuts, sliced

- 1 tablespoon of cornstarch

- 1/4 teaspoon of crushed red pepper flakes

- 2 teaspoons of ground ginger

- 1/2 cup of instant brown rice

- 3 tablespoons of soy sauce

- 2 ounces of hoisin sauce

- 1/2 bell pepper, sliced

- 3 ounces of broccoli florets

- 2 stalks of bok choy, sliced

Put the meat in a bowl. Season it with ginger and garlic. Cook the rice according to directions. In a bowl, combine the cornstarch, hoisin sauce, broth, and soy sauce. Heat a skillet over medium-high flame. Add oil. Cook the meat and red pepper flakes for 5 minutes while constantly stirring.

In another pan over medium-high flame, put the broccoli, carrot, and bell pepper. Sauté for 3 minutes while stirring frequently. You can add up to 2 tablespoons of water if you find the mixture too dry.

Add the bok choy and water chestnuts. Cook for 2 minutes while stirring often. Add the broth and cook for 2 more minutes while stirring constantly. Add the beef and cook for 2 more minutes. Pour this over the rice and serve.

Turkey Turnover Recipe

This recipe contains 9 grams of protein, 7 grams of fat, 13 grams of carbohydrates, and 155 calories per serving size of 2 pieces.

Prepare the following ingredients to make 24 servings of this dish:

- 1 envelope of dry onion soup

- 1 pound of ground turkey breast meat

- 3 tubes of low-fat refrigerated crescent rolls

- 1 cup of shredded low-fat cheese

Heat soup in a skillet over medium-high flame. Add the meat. Cook until the meat is browned while occasionally stirring. Stir in the cheese and mix until combined. Turn the heat off and set aside.

Separate the rolls and slice each piece of the triangle in half. Scoop 1 tablespoon of the meat mixture to each half of the roll. Fold the dough and seal. Arrange them on a greased cookie sheet. Bake for 15 minutes in a preheated oven at 350 degrees.

Turkey Bean Enchilada Recipe

This recipe contains 14 grams of protein, 3 grams of fat, 19 grams of carbohydrates, and 175 calories per serving size of 1 enchilada.

Here are the needed ingredients to make 4 servings of this dish:

- 4 fat-free tortillas

- 2 cups of skinless white turkey meat, cooked and cut into cubes

- 1 15-ounce can of pinto beans, rinsed and drained

- 1/2 cup of shredded low-fat Mexican cheese

- 1 cup of canned enchilada sauce, divided

- 6 scallions, green and white parts only, chopped

Put the scallions, turkey, beans, and 1/2 cup of enchilada sauce in a bowl. Mix until combined. Scoop 1/4 of the mixture to each tortilla. Fold the top, bottom, and sides of the tortilla to envelope the filling. Put them in a baking dish. Pour the remaining sauce on top and add cheese. Cover the pan. Bake for 20 minutes in a preheated oven at 350 degrees.

Zucchini Boat

This recipe contains 17.5 grams of protein, 7.5 grams of fat, 16 grams of carbohydrates, and 195 calories per serving size of 1 piece.

The following ingredients will yield 8 servings of this dish:

- 1 beaten egg

- 4 zucchinis, sliced in half lengthwise

- 1 pound of ground turkey breast

- 1/2 cup of chopped onion

- 3/4 cup of spaghetti sauce

- 1/4 teaspoon each of pepper and salt

- 1/4 cup of seasoned whole wheat bread crumbs

- 1 tomato, chopped

- 1/2 pound of sliced mushrooms

- 4 ounces of low-fat Mozzarella cheese

Thinly cut the bottom of each zucchini slice and scoop out the pulp. Set the pulp aside. Arrange the shells in a heat-proof dish. Cover the dish for 3 minutes on a high setting. Remove the liquid and set aside. Cook the meat and onion in a skillet over medium flame.

Once the meat is well-done, remove from heat and drain the

liquid. Put this in a bowl and add the breadcrumbs, beaten egg, spaghetti sauce, 1/2 cup of cheese, zucchini pulp, mushrooms, and tomato. Mix until combined. Scoop 1/4 of the mixture into each zucchini shell. Bake for 20 minutes in a preheated oven at 350 degrees.

Stuffed Cabbage Rolls Recipe

This recipe contains 15 grams of protein, 5.5 grams of fat, 16 grams of carbohydrates, and 174 calories per serving size of 1 roll.

You will need the following ingredients to make 6 servings of this dish:

- 1/3 cup of preferred whole grain rice

- 1 pound of 93 percent lean ground turkey

- 1 cabbage head, separate the leaves, wash, and blanch for 30 seconds

- 1 teaspoon of olive oil

- 2 teaspoons each of Italian seasoning and garlic powder

- 2 carrots, diced

- 1/2 onion, diced

- 2 cups of tomato sauce

Cook the rice according to package directions. Heat a skillet over medium flame. Add the olive oil. Saute the onions and carrots for 3 minutes while stirring often. Add the meat and cook until browned. Add the powders and seasonings. Mix well. Pour this over the cooked rice.

Mix thoroughly until combined. Scoop 1/2 of the mixture in every cabbage leaf. Roll the leaf to wrap the filling and seal the ends. Put them in a baking dish. Pour over the tomato sauce. Bake for 45 minutes in a preheated oven at 350 degrees. Set aside to cool for 5 minutes before serving.

14 - Bariatric-Friendly Recipes for Sauces, Spreads and Desserts

Squash Apple Bake

This recipe contains 1 gram of protein, 8 grams of fat, 17 grams of carbohydrates, and 133 calories per serving size of 1/6 of the recipe.

To make 6 servings of this dish, you will need the following:

- 2 teaspoons of ground cinnamon

- 2 apples, peeled, cored and sliced

- 1 tablespoon each of all-purpose flour and Splenda

- 1/2 teaspoon of salt

- 1/4 cup of melted butter

- 1 butternut squash, peeled and cubed

Mix the squash and apples in a casserole dish. Put the remaining ingredients in a bowl and mix well. Add this to the casserole dish and mix all the ingredients until combined. Cover the casserole dish. Bake for 50 minutes in a preheated oven at 350 degrees. Remove the cover and continue baking for 10 more minutes.

Creamy Jell-O

This recipe contains 1 gram of protein, 2 grams of carbohydrates, and 30 calories per serving size of 1/2 cup.

You will need the following ingredients to make 4 servings of this dish:

- 1 box of sugar-free Jell-O

- 8 tablespoons of Cool Whip Free

Prepare the Jell-O according to package instructions. Put in the fridge until set. Divide the set gelatin into 4 cups. Add 2 tablespoons of Cool Whip Free into each cup. Stir the ingredients in every cup and serve.

Chocolate Soy

This recipe contains 5 grams of protein, 1 gram of fat, 6 grams of carbohydrates, and 56 calories per serving size of 1/2 cup.

The following ingredients will yield 8 servings of this dish:

- 1/4 cup of hot water

- 1 packet of unflavored gelatin

- 1 1.4-ounce pack of fat-free and sugar-free chocolate fudge instant pudding

- 1 cup of cold skim milk

- 16 ounces of silken tofu, cut into cubes

- 1 tablespoon of cocoa powder

- 1/4 teaspoon of peppermint extract

- 1/2 teaspoon of vanilla extract

Dissolve the gelatin in hot water. Stir thoroughly so that no lumps are formed. Put in the fridge until set. In a bowl, combine the skim milk and instant pudding mix. Add the diced tofu.

Break up the pieces of tofu as you whisk the mixture. Transfer to a food processor and process until smooth. Slowly add the gelatin and process until the consistency is the same as a smoothie. Transfer to a glass dish, cover and put in the fridge. Serve once firm.

Fluffy Cottage Cheese

This recipe contains 22 grams of protein, 3 grams of fat, 24 grams of carbohydrates, and 220 calories per serving size of 1 cup.

Here are the needed ingredients to make 8 servings of this dish:

- 2 24-ounce packs of fat-free cottage cheese

- 1 8-ounce pack of sugar-free whipped topping

- 2 0.3-ounce pack of sugar-free gelatin

Mix all the ingredients in a bowl and serve. You can also add any fruit to the mixture to tweak the taste and increase its nutrient content.

Spicy Avocado Spread

This recipe contains 2 grams of protein, 5 grams of fat, 8 grams of carbohydrates, and 85 calories per serving size of 4 tablespoons.

Prepare the following ingredients to make 6 servings of this dish:

- 1/2 teaspoon of green Tabasco sauce

- 2 sprigs of cilantro

- 1 1/2 tablespoons of fresh lime juice

- 1 ripe avocado

- 1/2 green jalapeño, with the seeds removed and chopped

- 2/3 cup of cannellini beans, drained and rinsed

- 1/4 teaspoon salt

Put all the ingredients in a food processor. Process until

smooth and creamy. You can use this as dipping for vegetables or as chicken topping.

Yummy Pumpkin Mousse

This recipe contains 2 grams of protein, 4.4 grams of fat, 28 grams of carbohydrates, and 149 calories per serving size of 1 cup.

Here are the necessary ingredients to make 4 servings of the dish:

- 2 cups of sugar-free whipped topping

- 1 teaspoon of cinnamon

- 1 4-ounce pack of fat-free vanilla pudding

- Splenda, nutmeg, clove, allspice, and clove to taste

- 1/2 cup of skim milk

- 1 15-ounce can of pumpkin

Whisk all the ingredients in a bowl until creamy and smooth. Transfer to 4 cups and serve.

Peanut Powder Salad Dressing

This recipe contains 3 grams of protein, 2 grams of fat, 7 grams of carbohydrates, and 50 calories per serving size of 2 tablespoons.

To make 2 servings of this dish, you will need the following:

- 2 tablespoons of powdered peanuts

- 1 teaspoon of Splenda brown sugar blend

- 1/4 teaspoon each of Szechuan chili sauce and ground pepper

- 1/8 teaspoon each of sesame oil and garlic powder

- 1 tablespoon each of water and low-sodium soy sauce

Put all the ingredients in a food processor. Process until smooth.

Bean Spread

This recipe contains 11.5 grams of protein, 1.5 grams of fat,

34.5 grams of carbohydrates, and 198 calories per serving size of 2 tablespoons.

You will need the following ingredients to make 2 servings of this dish:

- 1 15-ounce can of pinto beans

- Salt and red or green Tabasco sauce, to taste

- Juice of 1 lime

Combine all the ingredients in a food processor and process until smooth.

Cucumber with Tzatziki Greek Yogurt Sauce

This recipe contains 6 grams of protein, 8 grams of carbohydrates, and 53 calories per serving size of 1 cup.

The following ingredients will yield 8-9 servings of this dish:

- 3 cups of fat-free plain Greek yogurt

- 2 cucumbers, peeled, seeded and chopped

- Salt and pepper to taste

- 3 tablespoons of lemon juice

- 1 garlic clove, minced

- 1 tablespoon cach of salt and minced dill

Place the cucumber meat in a colander. Season with salt. Let stand for half an hour. Drain excess liquid and pat them with paper towels. Put all the seasoned cucumber pieces in a food processor. Add dill, garlic, lemon juice, and black pepper. Process until combined. Transfer to a bowl. Put in the fridge for at least 2 hours. Drain excess liquid before serving.

Balsamic Dijon Mustard Dressing

This recipe contains 0 gram of protein, 26 grams of carbohydrates, and 85 calories per serving size of 1 1/2 tablespoons.

Here are the needed ingredients to make 4 servings of this

dish:

- 4 tablespoons of balsamic vinegar

- Pepper and oregano to taste

- 2 tablespoons Dijon mustard

Put all the ingredients in a bowl and mix well. You can use this as dressing for vegetables, chicken, or roasted salmon.

Protein Packed Pesto

This recipe contains 6 grams of protein, 5 grams of fat, 4 grams of carbohydrates, and 77 calories per serving size of 1/2 cup.

Prepare the following ingredients to make 4 servings of this dish:

- 2 garlic cloves, minced

- 1/2 cup of water

- 1/3 cup each of fresh basil and 1 percent cottage cheese

- 1 10-ounce pack of frozen spinach, thawed and chopped

- 1 tablespoon of olive oil

- 2 tablespoons of grated Parmesan cheese

Combine all the ingredients in a food processor. Process until smooth. You can serve 1/2 cup of the sauce along with poultry or fish dishes.

Light Alfredo Sauce

This recipe contains 5 grams of protein, 4 grams of fat, 5 grams of carbohydrates, and 71 calories per serving size of 1/4 cup.

Here are the necessary ingredients to make 8 servings of the dish:

- 1/2 cup of grated Parmesan cheese

- 1/4 teaspoon of black pepper

- 2 cups of skim milk

- 1 tablespoon of extra virgin olive oil

- 1/2 teaspoon of salt

- 3 tablespoons of all-purpose flour

- 4 garlic cloves, minced

- 1 cup of warmed chicken broth

Put oil in a pan over medium flame. Put the garlic and cook for a couple of minutes. Add the flour and keep on stirring until thick. Add the chicken broth. Slowly whisk the mixture until combined.

Add milk and mix well. Season with salt and pepper. Reduce the heat to low. Keep on stirring until smooth and thick. Stir in the Parmesan cheese. You can use the sauce as topping for chicken, pasta, and fish dishes.

15 - Conclusion

Thank you again for buying this book!

I hope this book was able to help you understand the basics on how to help yourself recover from the gastric bypass surgery. Let this book be your guide to a fitter and healthier you.

The next step is to try out the recipes found in this book and plan your meals, especially after your Gastric Bypass Surgery.

Finally, if you enjoyed this book, then I'd like to ask you for a favor. Would you be kind enough to leave a review for this book on Amazon? It'd be greatly appreciated!

Book 4 - Bariatric Cookbook

Delicious Post Weight Loss Surgery Meal Plans (Coping Companion, Before & After, Lap Band, Keeping Skinny)

1 - Introduction

Over the years, morbid obesity has become a major issue in the United States and other developed countries. The numbers of people who are morbidly obese are rising. Morbidly obese people have a body mass index of 40 kg/m2 or more. Oftentimes, these people fail to lose weight using the conventional methods.

As a last resort, doctors recommend to these people gastric bypass surgery to help them combat obesity. The demand for gastric bypass surgery is increasing due to its effectiveness in helping morbidly obese people. Many obese people are successful in losing weight and in maintaining their ideal weight.

There are seven different types of gastric bypass surgeries. These are the adjustable gastric banding (or laparoscopic banding), gastric sleeve procedure, gastric pacing, gastric balloon, the classic Roux-en-Y or proximal gastric bypass, biliopancreatic diversion with duodenal switch and the Magenstrasse and Mill procedure

Each procedure entails a different way of bypassing the stomach. Generally, the goal is to alter the digestive system by reducing the capacity of the stomach. The "new stomach" can only hold 1/2 to 2 cups of food as compared to 6 cups of food that a normal stomach can digest.

The health condition of the person and urgency of performing the procedure will dictate the type of surgery that doctors will recommend.

Most of the surgeries are irreversible. You cannot undergo another surgery to bring back the old way your digestive system works. A gastric bypass surgery is a lifelong commitment. Commitment includes changing your lifestyle and eating habits.

2 - Understand Your Digestive System before the Surgery

The digestive system composes of nine essential body parts to complete the process. Digestion starts in the mouth. Your mouth breaks down food by chewing and releasing enzymes. The swallowed food passes through the esophagus and reaches the stomach. The stomach releases gastric acid to further break down the food.

Do you know that the stomach can hold a maximum of 6 cups in every meal? Yes, that is the size of a football. When the digestive system malfunctions, you can eat more than this capacity of your stomach.

The stomach signals the gallbladder and pancreas when it cannot break down certain types of components in the food. The gallbladder for an instance produces bile to help the stomach break down fat. The pancreas secretes insulin and other digestive enzymes to break down sugar in your food.

If the pancreas does not produce the right amount of insulin and digestive enzymes, the sugar in food is stored as fat. The pancreas can increase blood sugar levels, which may lead to diabetes if constant delays in breaking down the sugar reoccur too many times.

When the stomach finishes the churning of food, it transfers the food to the small intestines. The small intestines have three major parts, the duodenum, jejunum, and ileum. The food passes through the duodenum where many of the minerals and vitamins in the food are absorbed. The jejunum and ileum further break down the food so that the body can absorb the other nutrients intended for the bloodstream.

The food goes to the large intestines. Water, electrolytes and other nutrients such as sodium and potassium are absorbed in the large intestine. When the body finishes classifying the nutrients found in the food you ate, it will transport the remaining material to the rectum. The body expels the waste through bowel movement.

Diarrhea and malabsorption occur when the stomach transports the food without digestion or partially digesting it. Since the small intestines cannot break down food without the gastric juices and other digestive enzymes from the stomach, bladder, and pancreas, they will immediately transfer the food to the large intestines.

The same goes through with the large intestines. The large intestines transfer the food to the rectum and the body expels the food through loose bowel movement.

Adjustable Gastric Banding

The first type of bariatric surgery is adjustable gastric banding or what commonly known as laparoscopic banding. This is a minimally invasive surgery. The surgeon attaches a binding in your stomach through small incisions on the upper abdomen. The banding is made of silicone and is adjustable. The most popular gastric banding is the Lap-Band under the Allergan and SAGB under the Ethicon.

The banding creates a very small pouch in the upper part of the stomach, which can only hold a ½ cup of food. This new pouch restricts the amount of food intake. You feel fuller even after eating a small portion of food.

Aside from minimal surgery invasion, another advantage of this procedure is its reversibility. You can ask to remove the banding when you have achieved your ideal weight and have the confidence to maintain your ideal weight for life.

Roux-en-Y or proximal gastric bypass

This is an irreversible surgery but many doctors recommend this to morbidly obese people because of its rapid effect. The procedure includes cutting a portion of the stomach and attaching this new pouch to the small intestine. The procedure creates a roux and a Y. It bypasses a part of the stomach. The new pouch can only hold 1 cup of food or lesser.

Other Gastric Bypass Procedures

Other procedures are gastric bypass sleeve, gastric pacing, and gastric balloon. Gastric bypass sleeve procedure involves cutting the stomach vertically and removing the fundus. The removal of the fundus shuts off ghrelin production, another type of hunger hormone. This procedure is irreversible since the operation involves removing a part of the stomach.

Gastric pacing aims to change the behavior of the digestive system, particularly the stomach. This does not require removal of any part or bypassing of the stomach. The procedure involves placement of an electrical pacing in the stomach. So far, this type of gastric surgery is still in the process of clinical study.

Gastric balloon procedure is placing a large object inside the stomach to restrict food intake. The idea of this procedure is to place the "balloon" inside the stomach for 6 months. During this period, the patient should learn to change his/her eating habits. The advantage of this procedure is its reversibility.

After 6 months, the patient undergoes another surgical procedure to remove the balloon. The disadvantage is the yo-yo effect on individuals who cannot maintain a healthy diet after the balloon removal.

The best procedure for weight loss depends on many factors. One factor you should consider is your health. You have to consult a physician about your decision to undergo gastric bypass surgery. You will take various tests such a BMI, blood test, cholesterol and other tests necessary to ensure a successful surgery. Complications might happen and you should be ready to face them.

Preparation before the Procedure

Gastric bypass surgery is a big leap on your part. There are things that you should do and prepare for. One consideration is the cost. The total cost of a procedure depends on your insurance coverage, the type of procedure and the fee of the surgeon and other health professionals involved.

Costs of the Procedure

Check your policy if it covers this kind of procedure to lessen the cost of surgery. A procedure without insurance may cost you approximately twenty thousand dollars or more. The longer you stay at the hospital the higher is your bill. One cause of staying longer in the hospital is health complications. To avoid these complications, you will undergo various lab examinations.

Aside from the cost of the procedure and the surgeon's fee, consider also the fee of other health professionals. Most likely, you might need the help of a registered dietitian. In some cases, you might need a psychologist to help you cope with the pressure of losing weight. Even if you plan your meals, consulting a dietitian is helpful.

Oftentimes, the emotional roller coaster of losing weight may take a toll on your emotional well-being. You feel like giving up or feel pressured into keeping up a diet after the surgery. A psychologist can help you unburden the stress related to a weight loss surgery. He can encourage and help you find your motivation to keep on going.

Commitment and Complications

The second factor to consider is commitment. A gastric bypass operation is a long-term commitment. The first year is somewhat easy because you see significant changes in your weight. Rapid weight loss is evident. You feel invigorated because the surgery is a success but the second year becomes a hard work.

The second year is the year of real hardship, where you need to maintain eating less food, and to continue eating at a slower pace. The question is "Are you ready for a life-long commitment, for a permanent change?"

You have to weigh the pros and cons of your decision. For

the next 10 years or for the rest of your life, you can never go back to eating fast food. You will never binge. You will never eat a lot of sugary food again. You must intake lots of food supplements to replace the nutrients lost due to decreased food portion size.

Aside from these kinds of commitments, you should be ready for the health complications during your recovery. Oftentimes, you will feel nauseated and frustrated because you cannot eat the food you usually have before the procedure.

You feel heart burns because of the reflux of gastric juices in your digestive system when you eat the wrong way. Every wrong decision you make means sufferings of unimaginable pain. Read the overview of gastric bypass procedure and the related complications before making a decision.

In short, before making the decision, you should be ready for these kinds of commitment and complications. Weight loss is not an easy journey. It has always been a tough one.

You should be ready to take this journey to improve your health and well-being. The only person who can make this journey a success is you. Other professionals can help you

along the way but the ultimate actor in a weight loss surgery
is you.

3 - Identify Your Weight Loss Goals

Losing weight before the surgery must have been your dilemma. No diet works for you. Exercises seem a taxing activity because of your busy life. Being busy should not be a reason to stop looking for ways to lose weight.

With the rising popularity of gastric bypass surgery, you begin to contemplate that this procedure may also work for you. You ask your colleagues or friends who have undergone the same procedure and gather information about the surgery.

Your weight loss journey starts the moment you contemplate in getting a gastric bypass surgery. At this point in your journey, setting realistic goals is an essential part of succeeding in losing weight. How realistic your goals should be? What are the considerations you should make?

Remember one thing. Your weight loss journey is different from other people. On some days, you may lose a lot of weight. There will be days when you reach a plateau and do not lose weight for a few weeks or so.

Sometimes, you may even gain a little weight. If you gain a pound or two, do not fret. Your body is a complex mixture of muscles, fat, and bones. The most intelligent scientists cannot understand why people gain weight even after so many rigorous diets and exercises.

Your body is different compared to others. Never compare their milestones with yours. If it takes two to three years to achieve your weight loss goals, just let it be. Perhaps, this is how your body copes with the gastric bypass procedure. Every person has a unique way of recovering from a major surgery and of losing weight after the surgery.

Just remember to continue with what you have begun. Your weight loss journey will be fraught with so many trials and complications. Focus on your goals. Never lose hope because if you do, you will slip back to your old self, resorting to food for comfort. Always remember your goal. Focus on that. Record what you ate and what you did to achieve your goal. You need a food journal to evaluate your progress.

How do you set up your real goal? Base your decision on the average weight loss related to the surgery. If you are going to choose lap band and the average weight loss after two years is 40% of the excess of the ideal weight, set your goals on this percentage.

For example, the excess of your ideal weight is 300 pounds. Normally, you would like to lose weight as much as possible and as soon as possible. However, this does not happen all the time. To achieve your goal of losing as much as 300 pounds, do it in installments. During the first year after the surgery, your goal is to lose 120 to 150 pounds.

On the second year onwards, losing the remaining 150 to 180 pounds is your next goal. If you do not achieve your goal in the second year, maintain your new eating habit and you will see the effect in the long term.

Talk with Your Loved Ones

Before you pursue the surgery, talk to your loved ones about your decision. Discuss with them about the changes you are planning to put in place in the house, especially if you are living with a partner, your kids or parents. They should understand your plans and be ready to support you. If there is one thing you need right now, it will be their encouragement and support.

Join a Support Group

A support group can encourage you at times when you think you cannot do it anymore. The members of the group can help you endure and resist the temptation of slipping back to your old self.

You can get lots of advice from these people because they are suffering the same way you do. With a support group, you can share your pain and emotional struggles. A support group can inspire you in sharing your struggles without feeling ashamed. A support group can be the people whom you can rely on if your loved ones are skeptical about your success.

4 - Things to do Before the Procedure

Preparation for a gastric bypass surgery may take long before the actual surgery happens. You will talk to different professionals such as the surgeon, registered dietitian, your psychologist and your insurance agent. There are other things that you need to do as part of the preparation stage.

First, ask your boss if you can have a longer vacation week for the surgery and for the recovery period. If your employer does not allow you to have an extended leave, you can always seek other employment opportunities but never compromise your chance of better and healthier body.

Seek other options to earn while you are recovering from the surgery. These situations should not stop you from choosing the right surgery.

Second, start eating the way you should be eating after the surgery so you can get used to it. Drastic changes will begin after the surgery so start conditioning yourself with these changes as early as before the surgery.

Third, learn the basic diet of a gastric surgery patient. This diet significantly differs from what you used to eat.

Fourth, prepare your kitchen. Throw away or remove every junk food in your fridge, freezer, and cupboards. Donate these foods to your friends, to your neighbors or to a charity.

The last thing you want is to be reminded of those junkies and feel the craving. Remember, after the surgery, your digestive system is an entirely different one. Its functions are restricted. Your hunger hormones are reduced. You should discipline yourself and discipline starts in your kitchen.

Change your utensils into smaller versions than the regular ones. Purchase measuring cups and other pieces of equipment to measure and weigh the food you eat. This may seem a bit ridiculous but you need to measure everything you consume. If you are eating in a restaurant or dining out, remember the standard sizes for each food.

Fifth, start a journal. This journal contains your daily meal plans, the things you do while you recover from the surgery and the things you plan to do to achieve your weight loss goal. A journal can help you keep track of your progress but never include a daily monitoring of your weight.

If you want to monitor your weight, do it on a monthly or quarterly basis. Daily or weekly monitoring of the weight you lost after the surgery will just frustrate and depress you, especially if your body has a slower pace of shedding those unwanted pounds.

A food journal can help you keep track of the food that makes you nauseous or triggers vomiting. During the course of your recovery, you will likely suffer diarrhea or dumping syndrome. Jotting down everything that happens right after you eat is important. This will help you avoid the food that triggers such complications.

Before going through the procedure, make sure you have prepared everything. Make sure you are ready for all the consequences, complications and changes that will unfold in the next few months.

5 - Things to do After the Procedure

The challenge begins after the surgery. Health professionals will still care for you until your recovery is complete. However, your role has the biggest impact on the success of your gastric bypass surgery.

The tasks of maintaining a healthy body are daunting but your commitment can help achieve your goals. The journey starts with understanding how your new pouch works. It continues by learning the basic diet of post-bariatric surgery and by knowing how to handle nutrition deficiencies.

Understanding your new pouch

After the surgery, the function of your stomach is still the same except that your stomach is smaller and can only hold a ½ cup of food. Weeks or months after the surgery, your stomach's capacity increases to 1 cup of food when the swelling subsides.

Over time, your new stomach stretches but only to a limited capacity. When your stomach heals and the swelling stops, you can eat solid foods but to a maximum of one cup a meal.

Avoid overstretching your new pouch. Eat in small portions and slowly. Eat the right food and drink the right liquids. This way you can overcome the risks of dumping and vomiting.

6 - Learn the Basic Diet of Post Bariatric Surgery

The success of gastric bypass surgery depends on your commitment to learning everything you need to know so you can achieve a healthy and skinny body. This includes learning the basic diet of post-bariatric surgery. All your meal plans are based on this basic diet.

The basic diet of post gastric bypass surgery consists of 50% protein, 25% fruits and vegetables and 25% grains (or starch). The portion size is also smaller than a regular balanced meal.

The protein comprises the bulk of your diet, sharing one-half of the daily food requirements. Your protein requirement is 8 to 10 servings or approximately 60 to 80 grams of protein. The total protein requirements include the protein supplements.

Vegetables are consumed in two servings a day. The same serving sizes are required for fruits. Grains and other starchy food have a combined two servings a day while fat is required at four servings a day.

Thus, if your food intake is 1 cup for each meal, your plate should contain ½ cup of protein-rich food, ¼ cup of vegetables and fruit and ¼ cup of starch or grains.

Variety is a concept of a healthy diet especially for people who have undergone bariatric surgery. For example, milk is high in calcium but lacks iron. To get iron from food, consider consuming meat or food that is high in iron. Strawberry is a good source of Vitamin C but a carrot is high in Vitamin A.

Calories and its function in your body

Every bit of food you eat, even the junk food, provides energy. You may get many calories from eating junk foods but these foods contain empty nutrients. The wrong notion about calories is it is bad for your health and body.

Actually, the optimum level of calories fuels your body and it functions. Consumption of calories more than the recommended amount is bad for you. No matter how small the amount is, excess calories pile up and become as stored fats.

The measuring unit of energy in food is kilocalorie (kcal) or just calorie. The number of calories in a food indicates the amount of energy you can consume for a given activity or in maintaining the necessary functions of your body. Generally, the more calories consumed, the more energy you can spend on activities.

Going back to why calories are important, protein, carbohydrates, and fats provide kilocalories of energy. For every gram of protein or carbohydrates, you get 4 kcal of energy. For every gram of fat, your body expends 9 kcal of energy.

Your body requires twice the amount of energy to burn fats as compared to protein and carbohydrates. That is why fat is consumed only in moderation. Protein, carbohydrates, and fats are macronutrients that are essential in keeping the body healthy. An omission of one of these nutrients can cause nutrient deficiencies.

Protein and its part of your recovery after surgery

Protein is important in the healing process after the surgery. It helps your body heal fast and build muscles. Protein keeps your immune system working properly, maintains healthy blood and provides more energy. Protein-rich foods also contribute other nutrients such as zinc, iron, B vitamins and thiamine.

The good sources of protein are meat, milk, eggs, cheese, yogurt and other food products from animals. Although plant sources contain protein, they are low in quantity and sometimes not as high quality as the protein found in food products from animals.

Legumes, soy, tofu, and nuts are good sources of protein that is plant-based. When eating, you eat the protein-rich foods first before consuming the other foods on your plate.

The challenge in consuming protein after the surgery is that your stomach may not be able to digest it. Some bariatric patients can cope with digesting protein-rich foods without any side effect. In case your stomach cannot tolerate protein-rich foods yet, you can supplement your protein requirements with whey protein.

Protein is essential in your diet. The recommended protein intake is 15 – 20 grams every meal or a maximum daily requirement of 80 grams.

Your sources can come from the food you eat but during the recovery weeks when eating solid food is intolerable, protein supplements are enough. As your new pouch heals totally, the recommended protein sources should come from food and supplements, not just supplements alone.

Carbohydrate and its job in keeping you healthy

Carbohydrates have a bad reputation when it comes to eating healthy. Many health experts advocate that carbs should be eliminated from the diet. The truth is carbs are essential to keeping the body healthy. The important thing is to distinguish the good carbs from the bad carbs for a healthy diet.

Good carbohydrates are high in fiber, and nutrients such as Vitamin A and folate and antioxidants. Fiber does not provide nutrients but is essential in keeping a good digestive system. Sources of carbohydrates are whole grain wheat, pasta, bread and, rice, vegetables, and fruits. The daily consumption is 100 grams minimum.

Sugar is a carbohydrate. Post-gastric bypass surgery diet includes foods rich in sugars that are either naturally added or substitutes to not more than 10 grams a meal. Sugar can be a natural component of an ingredient or artificially added into the food.

Watch out for added sugars when consuming packaged food. Sugar whether natural or added should be consumed in moderation. Examples of natural sugar are fructose and lactose. Lactose is the natural sugar in milk and milk products while fructose is found in fruits.

Aside from natural sugars, you can consume sugar substitutes and sugar alcohols in moderation. Examples of sugar substitutes are Saccharin and Stevia. Sugar alcohols have a lesser amount of calories but may cause bloating or diarrhea. Examples of sugar alcohols are sorbitol and xylitol.

Fat and its role in your body

Fat is good when consumed in moderation. Your body

needs fat to build cells and produce hormones. However, because of the many fad diets, people have misconceptions about fat.

Just like carbohydrates, there is a bad fat and a good fat. The good fats are essential in keeping your body healthy. Without these fats, some body parts may have difficulty performing their functions. One instance is when your body has a difficulty of supplying enough oil to your skin and hair. Without enough fats, your skin and hair become brittle and dry.

Another side effect of eliminating fats entirely from your diet is a nutrient deficiency. Some vitamins and minerals essential for body functions require fats. Fat-soluble vitamins are Vitamin A, D, E and K. Your body needs fats to break these vitamins to an absorbable level.

What are good fats and bad fats? The four major types of fats are monounsaturated, polyunsaturated, trans-fat, and saturated fats. Polyunsaturated and monounsaturated are healthy fats because these fats lower the bad cholesterol in the blood. Sources of these fats are olive oil, avocados, and some vegetable oils. Fishes are also good sources of monounsaturated and polyunsaturated fats.

Trans fat and saturated fats are bad for your health. Identifying these fats is easy. Trans-fat is present in processed food such as cookies and doughnuts while saturated fats come from animal meat sources such as chicken, beef, and pork. To avoid trans-fat totally, read labels of packaged food. Watch out for hydrogenated oils. These oils are trans-fat.

Alternatively, avoid eating processed foods. Labels may show that the processed food is trans-fat free even if the food contains less than ½ gram of trans-fat. This has something to do with government regulations and manufacturer's packaging.

Chicken meat, beef, and pork are good sources of protein. To minimize saturated fats in your diet, consume lean and organic meats. Remove visible fats when cooking meat. These fats are the real sources of saturated fats, not the lean meat. Alternately, you can eat vegetables that are rich in protein such as legumes.

Also, limit your daily intake of sodium. The daily maximum is 2,300 milligrams.

Reading Nutrition Labels

Buying packaged products such as cheese, milk and some canned goods is unavoidable. What you can do is to learn how to read nutrition labels. All packaged products have nutrition labels on them.

Look for the recommended serving size. Remember the three macronutrients when reading nutrition facts. Compare percentage daily values. The serving size describes how much calories and nutrients a serving contains.

Nutrients per serving are in percentage daily values and are measured using the standard measurement applicable to that nutrient. A percentage daily value of 5% or less is little while 15% or higher is a lot.

For example, a serving size of a packaged product gives a 440 kcal. The nutrient facts include 29% fats that composed of 21% saturated and trans fat and 36% sodium. The other nutrients facts include 18% carbohydrates with a sugar content of 6 grams and fiber of 16%. The protein content is 15 grams per serving that consists of 45% Vitamin A, 4% Vitamin C, 20% Calcium and 20% iron.

The food in the example is very high in fat since it contains 21% saturated fat. This is above the recommended 5% daily value. Avoid this type of product because it causes nausea and worsens dumping.

With regard to the sugar content, choose foods with less than 10 grams. Some people who have gastric bypass surgery report that they experience dumping when they consume more than 10 grams of sugar.

Although dumping complications vary from one bariatric patient to another, it is best to benchmark such claims. You wouldn't want to risk yourself with this complication because dumping has no cure. The only thing you can do is let it pass, which is a nightmare.

Using the food example, the sugar content is within the minimum level of 10 grams. The carbohydrate content is at an optimum level. Avoid candies, soda drinks, and other products with added sugar. Eat whole grains, vegetables, and fruits to ensure your carbohydrate intake is at the optimum level.

Protein intake is 60 to 80 grams a day. On the example, the food contains 15 grams of protein for every 300 grams. The packaged food is at the 80-gram level but is not enough. You need to add more protein. The packaged food is very high in sodium. If you have not eaten any food with high sodium content, consuming this food is acceptable.

If in case you experience nausea or feel the need to vomit, record it in your journal. Write all the nutrition details for future reference.

How to Handle Nutrition Deficiencies

After a gastric bypass surgery, the most common side effect is nutrition deficiency. Your stomach has limited capabilities to absorb nutrients from the food you eat because of the limited amount of food intake. The most common nutrient deficiencies are Vitamin A, C, B1, and B12, iron, calcium, folate, and zinc.

The signs and symptoms may include lack of coordination

and poor eyesight. It may also include slower metabolism rate, mood swings and difficulties in sustaining short and long-term memory. Malnutrition is also a common effect of bariatric surgery.

To address nutrient deficiencies and malnutrition after a surgery, eat a balanced diet and take food supplements. A regular blood monitoring can also prevent deficiencies and malnutrition. You and your dietitian can work it out if nutrition deficiencies occur while you are recovering from the surgery.

7 - Supplementing Your Diet

There are two considerations when taking your supplement. The first consideration is taking the right supplements. The second consideration is the time of taking them.

During the first two weeks after the surgery, you need protein supplements, regardless of the type of the gastric bypass surgery. The protein powder is dissolved or is included in your liquid diet as a protein shake.

On the third week onwards, you need multivitamins, minerals, Vitamin B12, calcium and Vitamin D in addition to the protein supplements. Your dietitian may require other supplements depending on your blood tests.

The multivitamins are in chewable or liquid suspension during the recovery stage. From week 10 onwards, you can intake tablets and non-chewable medicines. By this time, your stomach is used to solid foods.

Supplements are part of your daily diet even after your stomach has healed. Taking these supplements strictly can help you keep your body healthy for life. Multivitamins and other supplements help in regulating appetite and metabolism. These can help in controlling hunger and can help in absorbing nutrients from the limited amount of food you eat.

Remember, these multivitamins are supplements and are no substitute for a healthy diet. You should prioritize eating a balanced diet and gradually lessen supplements to a small quantity or as prescribed by your dietitian or doctor.

Protein Supplements

Fifty percent of your bariatric diet comes from protein-rich foods. Sixty to eighty grams of protein is the required amount every day. For the first few weeks after surgery, reaching this required amount of protein is almost impossible.

The only way to reach the 80-gram level every day during the first few weeks is through protein supplements. You need to build muscles and retain those muscles to help in making your surgery a successful one. You know that muscles need more energy, which means you need more calories for energy. More importantly, protein helps your stomach heals and recovers fast.

Protein supplements are abundant in the market. The problem is finding a good one that tastes good, is affordable and appetizing.

You should buy protein powder that provides a maximum of 30 grams of protein, 10 grams of sugar and 5 grams of fat for each serving. Each serving can be 1 tablespoon or 1 scoop, depending on the nutrient label. Always read the nutrition facts before using a supplement in your meal.

Nowadays, a protein supplement with the highest quality is the whey protein. This is a by-product of manufacturing cheese. Since this is a by-product of milk that contains lactose, choose whey isolates if you have lactose intolerance.

Whey isolates have lower lactose compared to the standard whey powder. Watch out for protein supplements with collagen. These have low protein contents and may not be sufficient for your required daily protein intake.

You can take 1 to 2 protein shakes every day. You can also include protein supplements in your desserts. Combine these supplemental foods with the main dishes and make sure you have eaten a well-balanced diet. Never be tempted to replace natural protein sources with supplements.

Multivitamins and Other Supplements

Aside from daily protein supplements, you need to take multivitamins, too. Your surgeon and dietitian might require you to take at least one multivitamin tablet a day. If they require more than just one, follow their instructions, especially if the blood tests turn out that you are experiencing severe nutrient deficiencies.

8 - Meal Planning and its Benefits

To most people, meal planning is a time-consuming activity. If you had done meal planning before your gastric bypass surgery and failed, it could be that you are doing it the wrong way. After your surgery, meal planning should be one of your priorities before you start your day.

A 25-minute meal planning at the start of your week is not a nuisance at all if you just give it a try. Every week, schedule meal planning and make it a habit. You will be surprised to learn that it is rather easy to do. Besides, you have to master the art of meal planning so you can be sure that you are eating the most nutritious food in your new pouch.

Meal planning has many benefits. The first benefit is saving precious time in thinking what to eat and not to eat. If you spend time thinking what to eat every day, you are wasting time.

However, if you devote at least a few minutes once a week, you can use your time for other activities. You do not need to rush to the grocery to buy certain ingredients. You do not need to thaw an ingredient for the last minute cooking.

The second benefit is adding variety to your meals. List

every meal that you usually cook for a week. You might be surprised to find out that in a week you are cooking the same meal all over again. With meal planning, you can introduce a new recipe in your meal. You can apply the principle of variety when preparing meals, or increase your chance of getting the necessary food nutrients that your body needs.

The third benefit is saving money. When you are done planning your meal for at least two weeks, you can list all the items you need to buy in the grocery. Perhaps, you can even find a bulk discount for buying bulk items or bargain items. You do not need to buy items that you do not use. No more impulsive buying, ever again. You can go to the grocery once a week and save time and fuel expense.

The fourth benefit is enjoying a stress-free meal. After the surgery, you have a few days off but you have to go back to your work soon. With meal planning, you do not have to worry what to prepare because you already have prepared your food for the week. Just get the food from your fridge, cook it or place it in a microwave and wait for your food while you relax and read your favorite book or watch the latest news.

The fifth benefit is enjoying the food you love to eat except that the ingredients are more nutritious. For example, your favorite is burger and fries. You do not need to forgo these foods. To make it healthier and friendlier to your new pouch than the usual burger and fries, try buying burger patties with less fat.

You can even make a healthier version of the patty such as making it with veggies as substitute ingredients. Instead of cooking it in oil, try using a nonstick pan to fry the patty. Alternatively, grill the patty for a different taste. For the bun, use whole grain. For the fries, instead of deep-frying, try baking it with olive oil, pepper, and salt as seasonings.

Meal planning is easy and fun. You can still eat your favorite food without compromising your healthy diet. You can use substitutes so you can still eat what you usually eat with a few modifications.

With meal planning, you can change your eating habits one step at a time. You can change your lifestyle and make your gastric bypass surgery a successful one.

Stock Your Kitchen with Nutritious Ingredients

Fruits, vegetables, meat, and grains should be part of your kitchen. Aside from these essential ingredients for cooking, buy herbs and spices.

Herbs are dried leaves and stems of plants. Examples of herbs are basil, bay leaves, oregano, coriander and lemongrass. Spices are dried seeds and bark of a plant. Examples of spices are pepper, garlic, onion, and paprika. Herbs and spices can help you spice up an ordinary food. These ingredients are also rich in vitamins and minerals that you need to combat nutrient deficiency.

Aside from these ingredients, nutritious oil for cooking is also an important addition to your kitchen. Olive oil, canola oil, and sesame oil are better alternatives than using lard or ordinary vegetable oil. Extracts should also be part of your cooking ingredients. Examples of extracts are lemon, vanilla, and almond extracts. You can use these extracts to flavor up baked goodies, drinks, and other main dishes.

Conclusion

A gastric bypass surgery entails major changes in your life. These changes include learning how to forgo your bad eating habits and changing your bad eating habits into healthier ones. You can start implementing these changes by stocking your kitchen with fruits and vegetables and by learning the basic diet of post-bariatric surgery.

9 - Coping with Complications and Other Health Issues

Like any other major surgeries, you might experience complications and other health issues. No matter how strict you are with your diet and how good you are at following orders from your surgeon and physician, you might still encounter complications more than once.

Stomach Pain, Nausea, and Vomiting

These are common sicknesses during the recovery phase. This might be due to your body's reaction to the anesthesia wearing off and your body's way of coping with your new pouch. After recovery, these might be caused by several reasons such as eating the wrong food in the wrong way.

Other reasons may include eating and drinking at the same time, eating too fast, swallowing without chewing the food thoroughly, drinking carbonated drinks and dehydration.

The risks of continued vomiting due to your carelessness may include obstruction in the opening of your stomach due to swelling, hernia and tearing apart of the incisions in your stomach and your abdomen.

Dehydration and nutrient deficiency may also be a risk if your vomiting continues. When vomiting persists even after avoiding the food, you should not eat and after taking all the precautionary measures, visit your doctor to determine what is causing it.

To avoid nausea and vomiting, eat slowly and chew your food thoroughly. Stop drinking carbonated drinks. Instead, drink lots of water and non-sugary liquids. Even if you have recovered from the surgery, it is best to become steadfast in your weight loss goals.

Constipation

Anesthesia and the pain medications you are taking while in the hospital may cause constipation. To deal with constipation, drink lots of liquid to help your intestines flush out the toxins in your body.

Move a lot. If constipation persists after hospitalization, insufficient drinking of fluids is a possible cause. It is normal to experience constipation during the recovery stage after the surgery because of the restricted intake of fiber.

Follow the recommended daily liquid intake. By the end of week 9, you should be drinking 6 to 8 glasses of water to keep you hydrated and to help your intestines do their job. You may use suppositories and stool softeners to help you alleviate constipation. Before using these stool softeners, consult your surgeon first.

By week 10 and onwards, you can include fresh fruits and cooked vegetables to complete your daily requirements of fiber. Consumption of fiber can help alleviate constipation.

Diarrhea

This is another complaint of most bariatric surgery patients. Reasons may include an inability of the stomach to absorbed fat, sugar substitutes, lactose intolerance and certain food intolerance. If you are experiencing 4 – 5 loose bowels in a day, visit your surgeon to see what is causing your diarrhea.

Do not attempt to cure your diarrhea by taking medicines. Remember, you have a digestive tract with limited capabilities. The standard medicines for curing diarrhea may not be applicable to you anymore. There is one thing you can do, though. Do not stop drinking fluids to compensate for the lost liquid in your body.

Dehydration

It can be caused by severe vomiting or insufficient drinking of liquids. Dehydration is normal a day or two after a gastric bypass surgery due to the difficulty of tolerating liquid. Common symptoms include parched lips, dry skin and eyes, dizziness, irritability and dark urine.

Drink lots of liquid. If you cannot tolerate plain water, spice it up with flavor. Just remember to drink sugar-free or low-calorie juice. You may also slurp a no-sugar ice-pop as desired. Use the same container to track your liquid intake. Fresh fruit juices are okay as long as they are diluted with water. Your juice drink should be half fruit juice and half plain water.

After day three of your surgery, you should be able to tolerate most types of liquid. If you cannot tolerate drinking liquids by this time, consult your surgeon.

Food Intolerance

After the surgery, food intolerance is normal because of the altered state of your stomach. Common symptoms include a feeling of stuffiness in your stomach as if foods are trapped in the opening of your stomach or an incessant pain that does not go away even after a few hours after eating. The best thing you can do is to record such feelings of pain whenever you eat and discuss these with your surgeon.

Foods such as bread, pasta, milk and milk products, and red meat might cause food intolerance. You should avoid eating these foods during the first 9 weeks. If you cannot help but experiment, just remember to record any incidence of food intolerance in your journal.

Lactose Intolerance

This could happen during the first 9 weeks. You may experience lactose intolerance after the surgery. This is due to the restricted ability of the stomach to produce gastric juices necessary to digest lactose.

If you suddenly develop intolerance to milk and milk

products, stop drinking them. Common symptoms may include bloating, stomach pain and diarrhea. If you are worried about calcium deficiency, you can always take supplements.

Dumping Syndrome

This is common to all types of gastric bypass surgeries. This happens when food moves fast from the stomach to the small intestines. Dumping syndrome is characterized by nausea, abdominal cramps, cold sweats, weakness, explosive diarrhea, fast heartbeat, dizziness and upset stomach. Two or three of these symptoms indicate you are suffering the feared dumping syndrome.

Food with high fat and high sugar content can cause dumping. Dumping syndrome may occur immediately after eating, as immediately as 15-30 minutes or 2-4 hours after eating. Dumping can last for hours depending on the amount of sugary or fatty foods you have eaten. There is no cure for dumping or no medicine to alleviate the pain. The only thing you can do is to lie down and wait for it to pass.

Not everyone with bypassed stomach experiences dumping.

Some may experience worse dumping syndrome than others are. Those who are unlucky, the dumping syndrome can become a chronic condition for the rest of their lives. Other people may only experience it temporarily.

They may also get the same reaction if they eat certain foods. Dumping syndrome may occur less as time passes since you already have a better understanding of how your new stomach works. You already know which food brings such occurrences.

Although every person's experience with dumping is unique, you can minimize dumping syndrome by avoiding foods with more than 10 grams of sugar such as chocolate, sports drink, frozen fruit with heavy syrup, and undiluted fruit juices.

Avoid consuming fatty foods such as hot dogs, French fries, and deep-fried foods. Remember the 5% to 15% daily values. If a food contains more than 15% of fats, it is considered as very high in fats.

On week 10 onwards, try eating more foods rich in fiber. Eat frequent small meals, instead of eating big meals for breakfast, lunch, and dinner. Include foods with complex carbohydrates and increase intake of food rich in protein and supplements.

Reactive Hypoglycemia

Reactive hypoglycemia happens after eating wherein your body's sugar level drops below the ideal level. The ideal blood sugar level is 4 mmol/L. Even if you do not have diabetes prior to your surgery, you may still experience this kind of complication.

When food with high sugar or fat content goes to the small intestine without being broken down properly, the pancreas produces more insulin to digest the food. As a result, your sugar level drops below the minimum. Symptoms may include hunger, clammy and cold skin, dizziness or shakiness, feeling of confusion and nervousness.

If you suspect reactive hypoglycemia, take your blood sugar level with a blood glucose meter. If the results are below the minimum, drink fast-acting sugar, approximately 15 grams. Examples of fast acting sugars are dextrose tablets, honey, and sugar dissolved in water. Wait for 15 minutes before checking your blood sugar.

If the level remains below the minimum, repeat drinking fast-acting sugar and check after 15 minutes. Alternatively, eat a small snack with protein and carbohydrates. This snack can consist of Greek yogurt with fresh fruits, peanut butter, and apple.

Do not eat foods with high sugar such as candies and cakes to elevate the level of your sugar. These foods have different sugar contents and may have an adverse effect on your blood sugar. Remember, reactive hypoglycemia happens because your stomach did not churn the food high in sugar and fat.

You can prevent hypoglycemia from happening. Do not skip meals and eat your meals on time. Do not drink alcohol and do not eat food with high sugar content and fat. As always, balanced diet is important.

Bloating

Gas in your stomach is normal. This happens when you "swallow" gas while eating and drinking. Soda drinks can also cause gas to accumulate in your stomach. This results in bloating.

This is painful and may overstretch your new stomach. You can prevent gas or bloating by eating slowly. Do not use a straw while sipping liquids. Avoid chewing gums. Remember to record in your food journal the food that causes bloating.

Hair Loss

Hair loss can be related either to poor nutrition or to the surgery. If hair loss happens right after the surgery, it is your body's response to the stress of undergoing the procedure. If it happens weeks after the surgery, the likely cause is nutrient deficiency such as iron or zinc deficiency. Hair loss may also be due to low protein intake.

Hair loss related to the surgery is not preventable. Besides, your hair will grow back once you have recovered. Hair loss due to nutrient deficiency is manageable. To prevent hair loss due to poor nutrition, make sure to eat foods rich in iron and zinc. Take protein supplements religiously.

Conclusion

Complications may vary from one person to another. You may experience worse complications compared to others. In some days, you feel fine. In other days, you feel worse than eating a single meal is a chore. Whatever complications you experience after your surgery, always consult your doctor about it.

Do not forget to write any symptom or complication you experience after drinking a certain liquid or eating a specific food. One way of keeping complications at bay is to become aware of what might happen and what will happen if you eat this and drink that. The only way to monitor is to keep a journal.

Complications are normal to some extent. If complications do not go away after three days, consult with your doctor right away.

10 - Week 1 to 2 after Surgery – Liquid Diet

The first few weeks after the surgery may be difficult since your food and liquid intake are restricted. After the surgery, you have to introduce food gradually to your new digestive system. While you are in the hospital for two to three days, or more depending on the type of the surgery done to you, your diet includes clear liquid and nothing else.

Day 1 and 2 after the surgery

It is a bit weird to drink liquids for breakfast, snacks, lunch, or dinner but it is the only "food" your stomach can tolerate as it heals. Clear liquid diet may include water, broth with different flavors, fruit juice diluted with water and no sugar added to it.

This type of diet will last for two days or up to a week, depending on your stomach's tolerance for new foods. Even if you are on IV fluid while in the hospital, you need to sip liquids to know if your stomach is working fine. During the clear liquid diet, try sipping at least 30 ml every 15 minutes on the first day and at least 60 ml of water every thirty minutes on the second day.

Oranges, lemon, strawberries, and blueberries are the examples of fruits that you can soak in the water to give flavor to your water. However, orange juices are not allowed during the first two weeks of your recovery.

Sample Clear Liquid Diet

When preparing broth for your liquid diet, make sure you remove the fats from the beef. Skin from organic chicken is okay to include when boiling it. Your new pouch cannot tolerate fatty foods yet.

You can add spices and herbs to spice the flavor of your liquid diet but limit it. You can add mint leaves in your tea or juice but do not eat the leaves. You can consume coffee and tea since these are considered clear liquids once diluted with water.

For breakfast:

- Mango, Apple, or Pineapple Juice diluted in water

- Broth (chicken or beef flavor)

- Gelatin without sugar

- Decaffeinated coffee

Snack

- No sugar clear liquid supplement

Lunch

- Beef broth

- Sugar-free gelatin

- Tea, no sugar with a few mint leaves for flavor

- No sugar popsicles

Snack

- No sugar clear liquid supplement

Dinner

- Broth (chicken, beef or pork)

- Flavored water no sugar

- No sugar popsicles

- Gelatin without sugar

Snack

- No sugar clear liquid supplement

On the second day, you can rearrange the order of this menu. It is a bit boring but you have to tolerate this diet. Besides, it only lasts for a few weeks or so until you can introduce solid foods to your diet. You can drink the liquids warm or cold, depending on your stomach tolerance.

Week 1 to Week 2 after the Surgery

Your first week starts after your doctor discharges you from the hospital. On the third day, assuming you stayed in the hospital for two days, try introducing full liquids to your clear liquid diet. Full liquid diet includes all the clear liquid diet in the first two days after surgery and full liquids.

A full liquid diet may include skimmed milk with 1% fat, hot dark chocolate without sugar, soya milk, buttermilk, low-fat pureed soups, thoroughly cooked cereals with a soupy consistency, juices diluted with water, no sugar puddings or custard, light yogurt without sugar and protein shakes.

You can include potatoes pureed in soupy consistency. Other vegetables that you can make into pureed soups include tomato, squash, carrots and other starchy vegetables that can be mashed and turned into pureed soup.

Full liquid diet lasts for two weeks. During these weeks, start taking your protein supplements. Protein helps your stomach heals fast. You can also start taking chewable vitamins and mineral supplements. Follow the doses your dietitian recommended you to take.

Remember to drink at least 48 ounces of liquid every day. Half of the required liquid intake daily may come from the clear liquid diet and the other half may come from full liquid diet. Sip the liquids and do not gulp. Take at least 20 minutes to finish a meal even if it is liquid.

If you start vomiting or nauseated after introducing full liquid diet, you can revert back to clear liquid for 24 hours. Then, proceed with full liquid diet wherein 70% consisted of clear liquid diet.

Gradually, change the ratio from 70% clear liquid and 30% full liquid to 50% clear liquid and 50% full liquid, until your stomach can tolerate full liquid. By the end of the second week, you should be able to introduce pureed diet. Otherwise, visit your doctor if you cannot tolerate pureed diet.

Examples of Full Liquid Diet

Here is an example of full liquid diet plan:

Breakfast

- Prepare oatmeal cooked in a ¼ cup of milk with 1 tablespoon of whey protein.

- Plain yogurt in small container with no sugar and low -fat content

Morning Snack

- 1 cup of protein shake

Lunch

- ¼ cup of Applesauce

- ¼ cup of Mushroom Soup with 1 tablespoon of whey protein

Afternoon snack

- ½ cup of protein shake

Dinner

- ¼ cup of cottage cheese, no fat

- Plain yogurt with 1 tablespoon of whey protein

Tips to Remember

Do not forget to drink water or any of the clear liquid diet mentioned earlier in between meals. You can also add chicken or beef broth in your meals. For breakfast, you can sip a ½ cup of chicken broth. On lunch, you can drink diluted juice drink. For meals with milk, use no fat to 1% fat or skim milk. Use salt sparingly, too.

Here is another example plan of a full liquid diet:

Breakfast

- Fruit Shake

- Plain yogurt

Snack

- Protein Shake

Lunch

- ¼ cup cottage cheese, no fat or low-fat

- ¼ cup of plain yogurt

- Diluted tomato juice

Snack

- Protein Shake

Dinner

- Chicken soup

- ¼ cup of applesauce

Snack

- Protein shake

After surgery, you might experience a temporary case of

lactose intolerance. You can follow a lactose-free liquid diet. Here is an example of a lactose-free diet meal plan:

Breakfast

- Chai protein shake

Snack

- Oatmeal cooked in 1 cup of soy milk, no sugar or lactose-free milk

Lunch

- Potato soup with 1 tablespoon of protein powder (1/2 cup)

- ¼ cup of diluted tomato juice

Snack

- Protein shake

Dinner

- Vegetable soup with 1 tablespoon of protein powder (1/2 cup)

- Applesauce measuring ¼ cup

Snack

- ¼ cup of Cream of Wheat

As you can see, the goal of a liquid diet is to eat meals and drink liquids in small portion, frequently. Follow this example so you can gradually prepare your stomach for the next stage, eating pureed diet.

11 - Simple Recipes for Applesauce, Fruit Shakes, and Protein Shakes

The above examples of the liquid diet include applesauce, protein shakes and fruit shakes. You can include these meals in planning your meals even after week 10. Here are the sample recipes for these meals.

Applesauce

This recipe calls for:

- Apples with approximate total weight of 4 pounds (around 10 apples)

- Lemon zest, 4 strips

- Lemon juice to taste (approx. 3-4 tablespoons)

- Cinnamon stick

- Sugar, dark brown, ¼ cup

- Sugar, white, ¼ cup

- Water (1 cup)

- Salt (1/2 teaspoon)

Procedure for cooking:

Peel, remove seeds and quarter the apples. Boil quartered apples in 1 cup of water with the lemon, sugar, salt, and cinnamon for 20 to 30 minutes or until apples are cooked and very tender. Remove cinnamon stick and lemon peel. Mash the apples for a coarse applesauce. Blend if you want a smoother, pureed consistency.

Tips to remember

Since you are a gastric bypass patient, you can use a sugar substitute such as honey. Alternately, cut to half the amount of sugar or remove the sugar. Applesauce is a good pair for yogurt and cottage cheese. Later on, you can pair it with savory dishes when you are eating more solid foods. Freeze the applesauce for later use. The recipe yields 1 1/2 to 2 quarts or approximately 8 cups.

Fruit Shake or Protein Shake

- Protein powder (1 scoop)

- Skim milk or low-fat milk or soy milk for a lactose-free diet (1 cup)

- Vanilla extract (1 teaspoon)

- Strawberry flavored no sugar drink crystals (1/2 packet)

- Crushed ice (1/2 cup)

Procedure for preparation:

Blend all the ingredients until smooth. For an alternative, use fresh strawberry. However, make sure that the pureed strawberry has no lumps and is blended very well. You can use other fruits for your protein shakes such as banana or apple. You can also use Greek yogurt or plain yogurt instead of milk.

Chai Protein Shake

This shake calls for:

- Protein powder, vanilla flavor (1 scoop)

- Chai tea, brewed (1/3 cup)

- Soy milk, no sugar (alternative: lactose-free milk) (1/3 cup)

- Pumpkin pie spice (1/4 teaspoon)

- Ice cubes (2 pieces)

- Peach (if fresh, ½ of the fruit; if frozen, 4 slices)

Procedure:

- Blend all ingredients until very smooth. You may add more ice cubes if you like.

Tips to Remember

If you do not want to prepare your protein shakes, you can buy pre-made shakes in the grocery. You should look for pre-made protein shakes that have 15 to 40 grams of protein and less than 5 grams of carbohydrates with fiber content already subtracted. For example, a protein shake contains 5 grams of carbohydrates, with 3 grams of dietary fiber. The carbohydrate content is 2 grams.

12 - Week 3 to 4 after the Surgery – Pureed Diet

On the third week until the fourth week after your surgery, you can introduce pureed or smoothie diet. Anything that is blended and turned into pureed food can be part of this diet. Foods may include blended fruits, meats, starchy vegetables, and even eggs. As long as no sugar is added to the smoothie and fat is kept to 1% for milk add-ons, you can include it in your smoothie diet.

You can only eat one-fourth cup of the smoothie food. Don't be disappointed. The most important thing is taking the slow way of healing your new pouch. You do not need to rush. Eventually, you will be enjoying other solid foods later.

You still have to maintain at least 1 liter of liquid intake, including clear and full liquids. You have to stay hydrated so that you don't experience constipation during these weeks of recovery. Do not forget to take your protein supplements and vitamins for a faster recovery and to avoid nutrient deficiency.

Example of Pureed Diet

Breakfast

- Cream of wheat (1/4 cup) with skimmed milk (4 tablespoons)

- Pureed fruit (2 tablespoons)

Snack

- Protein Shake (1 cup)

Lunch

- Poached small egg (1 piece)

- Melba toast (1 or 2 pieces)

Snack

- Protein Shake or Plain Yogurt (1 cup)

Dinner

- Pureed meat or mashed fish (4 tablespoons)

- Mashed potato with 1 tablespoon of protein powder (3 tablespoons)

- Mashed or pureed carrots (2 tablespoons)

Evening Snack

- Protein shake (1 cup)

How to Puree Food

You can puree fruits, vegetables, and meats. Fruits and vegetables are the easiest and meat is the hardest to puree. You can keep pureed fruits and vegetables for 8 months, provided they are frozen. Pureed meat and fish can only last for 10 weeks if frozen. However, to avoid contamination, eat pureed foods immediately or store them up to 2 weeks.

For 1/3 to 1/2 cup of cooked fruits, you need 2 teaspoons or 10 ml of liquid. Blending time is 15 – 45 seconds. This serving yields 1/3 to ½ cup of pureed fruits. A ¾ cup of cooked vegetables requires 3 teaspoons of liquid and yields 1/3 to ½ cup of pureed vegetables. Blending time is 1 – 2 minutes.

A ½ cup of cooked meat requires 4 tablespoons of liquid and yields 1/3 to ½ cup of pureed meat. Blending time depends on the consistency you want or until meat is smooth and no meaty fiber is evident.

For a thicker consistency, you can add starchy and mashed food such as potato, sweet potato or squash. For a thinner consistency, add milk, water for pureeing fruits or broth if you are blending vegetables and meat.

How to Prepare Pureed Meat

It is a bit unbecoming to blend meat for your meals but you have to tolerate it. This is a way of introducing solid food, despite its blended state, to your stomach. Do not worry. This diet only lasts for 2 weeks. There are times that your doctor may advise you to introduce soft diet even before your fourth week ends.

Pureed Beef

This recipe calls for:

- Lean beef, cut into 1-inch cube (225 grams)

- Water (1 cup)

- Salt and pepper to taste

Procedure for Pureeing:

Boil the beef cubes in a saucepan for 30 minutes or until tender. Let it cool after cooking and then freeze it in the refrigerator. Reserve the broth for blending. After freezing the beef, blend it with the broth until smooth. Add salt and pepper to taste. Place it in a sealed container, leaving a few inches space as room for expansion. Label your beef puree.

Pureed chicken or turkey

This recipe calls for:

- 500 g of chicken or turkey with skin and bone intact

- 2 cups of water

- ½ teaspoon of thyme (or a few leaves of lemongrass)

- Salt and pepper to taste

Procedure for Pureeing:

Cook meat in a saucepan with the leaves of lemongrass until chicken or turkey meat separates easily from the bone. Let it cool. Disregard lemongrass. Cut into pieces and blend with the broth, thyme, salt, and pepper. Properly label your pureed chicken.

You can also add vegetables and spices when cooking the meat. Blend the meat with the vegetables with a flavorful pureed chicken or beef.

Legumes Puree

Legumes are packed with vitamins, minerals, and protein. These can be protein substitute if you are following a vegetarian diet. This recipe calls for:

- 1 cup of legumes of your choice

- 8 cups of water

- ½ teaspoon cumin powder

- Salt and pepper to taste

Procedure for pureeing:

Boil 1 cup of legumes in a saucepan with 3 cups of water for 2 minutes. Soak the legumes overnight. Drain the following morning. Add 5 cups of water and cook for 45 minutes to 1 hour. You can also use a pressure cooker to reduce the time of cooking. Remove from heat and let it cool. Blend the legumes with ¾ cups of the vegetable broth. Place in a container and label it. Freeze for later use.

You can use canned legumes for this recipe. Just blend and eat. Watch out for high-sodium content and always read the nutrient labels.

13 - Week 5 to 9 after the surgery – Soft diet

On the fifth until the ninth week, introduce soft foods in your diet. The key is to introduce gradually the solid foods into your existing diet. If your stomach cannot tolerate soft foods, go back to the pureed diet for a few days then start introducing soft food again.

This takes a trial and error to know what your stomach can or cannot tolerate. Just remember to write everything in your journal so that you know which foods to avoid and which foods to eat.

This is the time to start thinking what foods are nutritious to consume. You can now replace or reduce the number of the supplements you are taking with those nutritious foods. This is the week to start eating a balanced diet albeit a slow one.

The food that you can eat in this phase of your recovery can include ground meat to ground fish, vegetables cooked thoroughly and fruits. You can still include smoothies. Always remember to drink lots of water throughout the day.

Examples of Soft Diet

Day 1 – 80 grams of protein

Breakfast

- Fruits of your choice, fresh or canned (1/4 cup)

- Ricotta cheese (1/4 cup)

- Bran flakes with a sprinkle of cinnamon powder (1 tablespoon)

Snack – Morning

- Protein Fruit Shake

Lunch

- String Cheese (1 piece)

- Bean soup (1/2 cup)

- Melba toast (1 piece)

- Snack – Afternoon

- Yogurt or protein shake

Dinner

- Chicken soup (2 ounces)

- Thoroughly cooked vegetables (2 tablespoons)

- Mashed potato or carrots (1/4 cup)

Snack – Evening

- Tuna pita (1/4 cup tuna, light mayo, and pita bread)

- Protein Shake

Take note: Pita bread must be whole wheat and limit your mayo to 2 tablespoons.

Day 2 – 65 grams of protein

Breakfast

- Omelet using 1 egg, 2 tablespoons of diced ham (or cooked meat) and 1 tablespoon shredded cheese, low-fat

Snack – morning

- None (or plain yogurt)

Lunch

- Ground beef with gravy, low-fat

- Well-cooked broccoli (or any vegetable of your choice)

- Fruit cocktail in its own juice

Snack – afternoon

- Pudding or protein shakes (if protein requirement is not met)

Dinner

- Baked fish (3 ounces)

- Beans, thoroughly cooked (1/4 cup)

- Mashed potatoes (1/4 cup)

Snack – evening

- Milk, low-fat (1 cup)

14 - Beyond Week 10 – the New and Healthier You

If you think week 1 to 9 is the hardest, think again. The most difficult part of a gastric bypass recovery is week 10 onwards. By this time, your stomach has healed and you can tolerate most of the solid foods. The urge to try and eat the foods you usually eat before the surgery becomes stronger. You feel confident that you can make the right decisions when it comes to eating healthy.

When you think you are doing it right, your decision fails you. If it happens to you, do not despair. You make mistakes. Every one commits them. Learn from your mistakes to strive in achieving a better and healthier you.

Change in lifestyle is the key to the success of a gastric bypass procedure. This includes changing the food you eat, portion sizes, the type of food, exercise habits and the way you are chewing your food. Post gastric bypass diet is a transition from a liquid diet to soft solid food. It includes the transition from eating junk foods to eating nutritious foods.

Make eating healthy a lifelong commitment. You need to

understand the different components of what consists of a nutritious food.

Post gastric bypass diet is an entirely different diet because you need to eat smaller portion sizes of the food than you used to eat. It involves chewing your food thoroughly to make digestion easier for your smaller stomach. Since serving sizes are smaller, your stomach and body absorb fewer nutrients than before the procedure. This requires a lifelong intake of vitamins and other supplements.

Learning the Different Cooking Methods

Cooking is an art but it also involves a systematic method of food preparation. Cooks invented recipes so other people can cook the same way they do. Shortcuts and experimentation are acceptable when you are cooking. However, when you want the same result as that of the recipe, you should follow the exact ingredients and instructions.

Every recipe involves different cooking methods. Each method yields different cooked foods. In a recipe, you might read or hear the words broil, braise and sauté. If you are a beginner in cooking, these words may seem similar but these cooking methods are different.

The recommended cooking method for the meat of land animals is dry cooking. Dry cooking methods include grilling, sautéing, roasting, broiling, baking and rotisserie cooking.

Dry cooking retains moisture in the meat. This cooking method is recommended during the first three months after the surgery when food tolerance is very low. This cooking method makes the meat and fish easier to chew, swallow and digest.

The most common dry cooking is sautéing because of its short preparation time. The method of sautéing is cooking food in a pan with a minimum amount of cooking oil. Pre-heating is a requirement before putting oil and before cooking the food.

This method is quick and easy. It takes only 7 minutes and requires slicing the meat into thin strips. While sautéing, do not walk away from the stove. If you walk away for a few minutes, you might burn the food.

Rotisserie cooking is rotating the food over dry heat while

cooking. Grilling is cooking food with heat from below with a charcoal or flame. Roasting is cooking food in a dry heat using fat or cooking oil. Broiling is cooking food with heat from above the food. Grilling, roasting, and broiling are slow-cooking dry methods.

These methods take a minimum of one hour of preparation time. You can use these methods if preparing a weekend party or gathering where you have enough time to prepare the foods.

The second cooking method is moist cooking. This method involves boiling, deep-frying, pan-frying, stewing, poaching, and braising. Stewing is cooking food cut into small pieces in a pot with liquid.

The food is cooked on a low flame with the lid on the pot. Braising is similar to stewing except that food is cooked with a minimal amount of liquid in an oven. Boiling is cooking the food in liquid under extreme heat. Poaching is cooking food at a simmer point.

Food Safety is Important

There are times that you cannot eat everything on your plate. You do not need to fill your stomach to a brim and that you should listen to your fullness signals. To avoid wasting food, you can preserve leftovers for later consumption. When you think you cannot eat everything on your plate, place the leftover in a sealed container and freeze the food.

Do not let the food sit for more than fifteen minutes or exposed to avoid contamination or germs getting on the food. For cooked food, consume the leftover within 24 hours to 3 days. Label your container when the leftover food is placed in the fridge so you can track the date and know how many days or hours have passed since the cooking.

Measure Everything

You have learned throughout this book that you should weigh your food and measure your liquids. The thing is how do you measure food?

There are different types of ounces in measuring weight and

volume. Fluid ounces are used to measure all kinds of liquid that literally pours such as water, broth, vinegar or milk.

In some recipes, ounces are used to measure weight but this measurement is not the same as fluid ounces. If you are not familiar with the English metric, you can always convert the measuring unit into the standard unit of measurement.

For example, you see a recipe that requires 3 ounces of milk. This means you should use fluid ounces and use a measuring cup for liquids. If you see an ingredient indicating 3 ounces of chicken, you should use weighing tools to measure solid food in ounces. Other recipes use the standard metric system, which is easier since most kitchen measuring tools are in standard metric.

To make measuring easier and faster, buy two sets of measuring cups and spoons, one for measuring liquid and one for measuring dry and solid food. You should also have a small weighing scale to measure food in grams.

In measuring flour, sift first before measuring. Flour tends to compact when packed in the bag. Sifting removes the compactness of the flour. The level measurement means you have to remove the excess ingredients by leveling the measured food with a measuring cup. You can do this using a knife or a spoon to level the ingredient with the cup.

The packed measurement means you have to press down the ingredients into the measuring cup. The unpacked measurement means you just scoop an ingredient and let it as is. Food with smaller cuts tends to have more contents than with food cut into bigger cuts.

Conclusion

Learn to cook so you can choose the ingredients in your food. You can substitute unhealthy ingredients with healthy ones. You may not learn cooking immediately but making the effort to learn how to cook will pay off.

To create a daily meal plan, choose 2-3 servings of protein-rich food, 2 servings of fruits and vegetables and 2 servings of grains or starchy food for every meal.

15 - Simple Breakfast Ideas

Breakfast is the most important meal of the day. So, never skip one. Eat a hearty meal to start your day. Here are sample breakfast ideas you can include in your daily meal plan. Just remember the basics, 50% protein, 25% fruit and vegetables and 25% grains or starchy food.

Toast and Fruit

- A slice of toast with 1 tablespoon of peanut butter

- Scrambled eggs with shrimp

- Small banana

- Berry Parfait

Start your day with a low-fat no-sugar yogurt (1/2 cup). Add cereal (1/4 cup) and 3 slices of strawberries.

Savory Crackers

- Ryvita crackers (2 pieces) or English muffin (1/2)

- Tomato (1 slice)

- Cottage cheese (1/4 cup)

- Pepper

- Egg Wrap

Sauté 1 slice of ham (diced) and 2 slices of tomato (diced). Add one egg. Cook for 1 minute. Roll egg scramble in a whole wheat tortilla wrap. Eat half of the egg wrap and re-frigerate the remaining half for tomorrow.

Fruity Wrap

Use a whole wheat tortilla wrap. Spread almond butter (2 tablespoons). Top it with applesauce (1/4 cup) and a pinch of cinnamon. Eat half of the roll and refrigerate the rest. Consume the other half for tomorrow.

16 - Easy Lunch Choices

With your busy life, forgetting lunch is a common occurrence. Stop this nasty habit and start preparing your lunch beforehand. You can bring with you a hearty sandwich or tortilla wrap for a quick but satisfying lunch. If you are up early or have time to prepare food in the evening, you can cook your food for lunch, freeze it and then just heat it when you're ready to eat lunch.

Cheesy Quesadilla

Use 1 small tortilla wrap, whole wheat. Top it with tomato (2 slices), spinach leaves without stem (6 pieces) and shredded fat-free cheddar cheese (1/4 cup). Fold the tortilla wrap in half. Bake the wrap in the microwave oven until the cheese melts.

Sandwiches for Lunch

Lightly spread a toasted English muffin with 1 teaspoon of low-fat mayonnaise. Top ½ of it with light cow cheese and smoked salmon (1/4 cup), capers (3 pieces), and chopped spring mix salad (1/2 cup). Alternately, use hummus (1/4 cup) and 3 slices of cucumber. Sprinkle salt and pepper to taste.

17 - Fast and Easy Dinner Options

Most of the times, eating dinner seems a chore. No matter how tired you are, fix yourself a quick dinner. Your stomach needs food to grind even if it is so small. It still releases hunger hormones and it needs something to grind on while you sleep.

Burger and fries

Who says you cannot enjoy your favorite burger and fries? You still can as long as you use a low-fat burger or a vegetarian patty. You can make the patty when you are not busy and have time to prepare it. Use a whole wheat burger bun (small) and top it with a ½ burger patty and spring mix salad. Skip the mayo. If you cannot skip it, use light mayonnaise. Oven-bake 4 fries to complete your dinner.

Breaded Chicken

Thaw 2 ounces of chicken, sliced into small cubes. Coat the chicken with crushed bran buds. Bake until the chicken is cooked. Serve it with tomato and cucumber (1/2 cup). For extra flavor, toss the tomato and cucumber salad with balsamic vinegar.

Chili

Prepare a ½ cup of salad mixed greens and chili (1/2 cup). Add sour cream in low-fat (1 tablespoon) and shredded cheese. Limit cheese to a sprinkle.

Stir-fry Seafood

Stir-fry shrimp (4 pieces) and vegetables (1/2 cup) in a teaspoon of canola oil. You can add peppers and mushrooms. Top the stir-fried seafood in couscous (1/4 cup) and a dash of soy sauce in reduced sodium content.

Sample Homemade Burger Recipe

If you are craving for burger and fries, use this recipe to make your burger patties. Store leftover patties and use them on other occasions. Preparation time is 10 minutes. This recipe yields 4 servings (4 ounces for each patty).

This recipe calls for:

- Turkey breast (1 pound, ground)

- Ginger root, peeled, chopped (1 teaspoon)

- Garlic, chopped (2 teaspoons)

- Sesame oil (1 teaspoon)

- Fresh mushrooms, chopped (1/2 cup)

- Onion powder (1 teaspoon)

- Black pepper (1/4 teaspoon)

- Soy sauce (1 tablespoon, low sodium content)

Procedure:

Preheat oven (350 degrees). Spray baking sheet with non-stick cooking spray. Combine all ingredients in a bowl. Form 4 patties and place them on the baking sheet. Bake the patties for a total of 15 minutes. Bake each side for 7 ½ minutes. Alternately, you can grill the patties.

18 - Tips to Keep a Skinny Body

Start your day with a smooth food. Gently prepare your new pouch with the new day ahead with yogurt and fruit smoothies. Fruits contain 80% water so digestion is easy for your stomach. Include protein powder in your shake for your daily protein requirements.

Include easy-to-prepare egg dishes for additional protein requirements. An egg is packed with protein, low sodium content and various vitamins and minerals. You can fry it in olive oil, poach it or boil it.

You can scramble it and add veggies for a morning omelet. You can use non-fat butter to make it tasty for many people who had undergone gastric bypass cannot tolerate eggs. Furthermore, it is so easy to prepare.

You can also begin your day with whole grains but dilute it with water while cooking. Whole grains have a tendency to expand when eaten. Since your pouch is smaller, you might experience extreme fullness that may lead to vomiting.

Cook lunch and dinner using one-dish principle. This means looking for a recipe that contains all the macronutrients that you need. For example, a recipe of chicken enchilada contains protein, calcium, carbohydrates and other essential nutrients.

Chicken contains protein. If you include cheese in cooking, you get your calcium requirement for the day. The enchilada sauce contains vitamins and minerals because of the tomato ingredients.

Toss in your favorite salad ingredients for a hearty afternoon snack. Just remember to choose low-fat mayonnaise or dressing to minimize consuming fatty foods. Alternately, use lemon, a tablespoon of olive oil and a dash of salt and pepper for a simple salad dressing.

The Order of Eating Your Food

You have to follow a strict code of eating healthy to maintain your weight and to minimize risks of dumping syndrome. Even if it means repeating a set of a meal for the next month or so, you will have to follow a strict diet of nutritious food. You will have to take supplements and eat your food in a particular order for the rest of your life.

In eating your food, you eat the protein first. Protein is the most important nutrient. Even if you did not finish your meal, the important thing is you got your protein require-ment first. Fifty percent of your daily nutrition requirement comes from eating protein food and taking protein supple-ments.

After eating your protein, eat the vegetables and fruits in your meal. These can be in the form of a smoothie, soup or solid cooked food. The last is the starchy food or grain. If you feel full after eating your veggies and fruits, you can stop eating. You do not need to eat everything on your plate.

Meditative Eating

Is there such a thing as meditative eating? Yes, there is. Meditative eating, in other words, mindful eating, is con-necting with your body's signal for fullness and hunger. It is paying attention to your new stomach. Meditative eating lets you eat leisurely and be mindful of the serving portions of every meal. It helps you in achieving your goals and min-imizing risks of nausea and dumping.

Meditative eating consists of five components. The first component is eating slowly. Give at least 20 minutes or more but not exceeding to 1 hour to finish one meal. Chew your food thoroughly.

The idea is to chew your food 20-30 times. Do not rush and put down your spoon and fork in between bites. The best time to practice mindful eating is when you are slightly hungry. Thus, eat on time. Schedule your mealtime and follow it strictly.

The second component is persistence. You will have to do meditative eating for the rest of your life. Doing it once or twice is not enough. Make it a habit. Before you know it, you are doing meditative eating automatically.

The third component is openness. Become aware of what is going on with your body, particularly with your stomach. Sometimes, meditative eating can be a relaxing endeavor. Sometimes, you feel agitated especially if you feel your stomach is not doing okay.

The fourth component is to forget all criticisms from other people. These criticisms create negative feelings. Morbidly obese people, like you, are prone to judgmental comments from other people who can never understand how you feel. Most of the times, when you eat a meal, you would think if the food you are eating will not gain you a pound or will the food you eat will help you lose weight.

Stop these thoughts. Start thinking that eating is part of your success in losing the weight you hated since you hit that 40 BMI. Eating is a nutritious habit that will help you in losing more weight because you need to sustain your body's need.

The last component is doing one thing at a time. If you are eating, concentrate on eating. Do not watch TV or read a book while eating. It's okay to listen to classical music or your favorite sounds while eating. Listening to a relaxing music may even help you enjoy your food and chew slowly.

After the surgery, you will face big changes, including on how you view food. With meditative eating, you can handle these changes without being overwhelmed. Use your inner and outer wisdom to practice meditative eating and experience a positive impact on the gastric bypass operation in your life.

Outer wisdom refers to your basic knowledge of gastric bypass, to professional help from your surgeon and dietitian and experiences of other people with the same situation as you are.

Reading a book similar to this is also considered as an outer wisdom. Inner wisdom is your connection with your basal needs, your hunger and fullness signals and your stomach's reaction to the food you eat and drink. This also includes the feelings you experience before and after eating, emotionally and physically.

Aside from wisdom, it is important to appreciate the quality of the food you eat, instead of quantity. This is another aspect of meditative eating that you should practice. Perhaps, your parents have ingrained in your mind that everything you place on your plate should go to your stomach.

No food should be wasted. While this is the right thing to do, with your current state of a smaller stomach, you do not need to eat everything. To avoid wasting food, eat your meal one at a time. Just remember to eat the protein first before eating the vegetables and fruits. If you cannot really finish what you have prepared, freeze the remaining food and eat it for your next meal.

As you practice meditative eating, you will get a better understanding of how your stomach works. You will be able to estimate the amount of food you can eat in one sitting. Quality is the amount of nutrition you can get from a meal despite its smaller portion size. It refers to the freshness of the food, not processed or frozen to keep its shelf life.

Take Note of Portion Sizes

While eating slowly can contribute to losing weight and keeping your body free from complications, you should also be mindful of the serving sizes of your meals. It is useless to eat slowly and chew your food thoroughly if you are eating more than the recommended portion sizes for your new stomach.

Make it a habit of measuring and weighing the food you eat. Over time, you feel confident how a ½ cup of cereal or grains will look like in a bowl. There is nothing wrong if you know you can measure your food without needing a weighing scale. From time to time, check your measurements with the weighing scale and measuring cups and spoons.

However, there will be times that measuring becomes impractical, especially if you dine out occasionally or eat at a party. It is best to know a few guidelines in measuring portion sizes without actually using any measuring tool.

Drinking the Right Way

Water is an essential part of your post bariatric surgery. It helps your body distribute the necessary nutrients derived from the food you eat. Water keeps you hydrated, making your body function at an optimum level. Despite its importance, drinking the right way after the surgery is important.

Stop drinking at least 30 minutes before any meal. This will give your stomach enough time to do its work of distributing the water to your body parts. Resume drinking water at least 30 minutes after a meal.

Avoid drinking water and eating a meal at the same time. Water will push your food immediately to your intestines, making you eat more than usual. The worst thing is experiencing dumping syndrome.

There should be no alcohol during the first 10 weeks of recovery. Your new pouch is swollen and healing during these weeks. If you can manage, remove drinking alcohol altogether. Too much alcohol in your diet will not be good for your new stomach.

Avoid drinks with more than 10 grams of sugar. Many persons who had bariatric surgery notice that they suffer vomiting and dumping when they consume drinks with more than the 10-gram mark. Use natural sweeteners such as honey. You can use a sugar substitute to sweeten your drinks but use it sparingly. If you are bored with plain water, you can always spice up your drink with ginger, lemon or mint.

Sip your drinks. Do not gulp. Your stomach might rebel. Drinking in one gulp may cause vomiting. The worst thing is gulping may stretch your stomach. Gulping on a regular basis will hurt your stomach and may cause the staple and incision to open.

Drink the recommended water intake every day. During the first few weeks, your water intake may be limited to 1 liter a day. Every week, increase your water intake until you reach 2 liters a day.

Eating out, a possibility or not?

There would be times that you cannot help but eat out, either at a restaurant or at a get-together party or gathering. Gastric bypass surgery might have brought drastic changes in your life but it does not mean you give up all the things you enjoy before the surgery.

You cannot decline a date out with your loved ones, all the time. From time to time, you can still indulge in the pleasure of dining out. Your surgeon can even give you an identification card indicating you have undergone a gastric bypass surgery and that you need smaller serving sizes and healthier food servings that the restaurant is serving.

The employees of the restaurant can make changes for you. Some may ignore your request. Fortunately, more restaurants now are serving nutritious foods.

Surviving in a restaurant or fast food should not be a nightmare. Remember these tips and you can survive eating at a restaurant or fast food without experiencing any of the complication. Do not order food that indicates deep-frying or has a creamy sauce or crispy filling as part of the description. Most likely, these foods are high in fats. When dining out, you can request to place your salad dressing on the side.

Opt for veggie alternatives instead of an all-meat menu. For pizza restaurants, order a pizza with thin crust and more vegetables. Skip the pepperoni and sausages. For pasta menus, ask for the whole wheat variety with red sauce, instead of creamy white sauce.

In burger joints, you can order grilled patties instead of fried. When dining out in an Asian restaurant, order steamed veggies and meat. Skip fried rice. Instead, request for brown rice. Use chopsticks to slow you down when eating.

Keeping a Food Journal

During the weeks of your recovery and even after recovering and achieving your ideal weight, keep a food journal. A food journal is your lifelong tool in maintaining your weight. You should not stop writing in your journal. According to research, people who maintain a food journal lose more weight than those who do not keep one.

Jotting down everything you eat, a number of calories consumed can help you track down if you are eating right. This food journal can boost your confidence. It can improve your understanding of the reason you are eating.

Writing down your emotions and your cravings can help you evaluate what you really feel. It can help you think of alternate ways to divert your attention away from these cravings.

During the time when you are trying to achieve your weight loss goals after the surgery, cravings will become normal occurrences. Writing these cravings down in your journal will help assess your true feelings and what situations bring such cravings.

A food journal can help you plan your daily meals. You can write down your plan early in the morning as you sip your first no-sugar coffee or low-fat milk of the day. Planning what you will eat during the day is one-step away from your success. If you write down all symptoms and complications after eating a certain meal, you can identify specific patterns on how your stomach reacts to food.

Your food journal is not only for your own benefit. Your surgeon and dietitian can review your food journal to see how you are doing, especially if the supposed results of losing optimal weight are not favorable.

You can create a template for your food journal, which you can fill up as the day progresses. On the heading part, you can place the time of the day such as breakfast, lunch, dinner, morning snack or afternoon snack. You can also include the specific time of the day.

You can format it in a table form wherein the first column contains your meal plans and the corresponding measurements for each food to eat and liquid to drink. You should include the supplements you are taking or any exercise regimen you are following.

On the second column, write the remarks or any effect of the food or liquid you have consumed. These remarks may include any nauseous or vomiting episodes, stomach pain or cramping. Other information should include calorie intake, protein, and ounces of liquid consumed.

Alternatively, you can use an online food journal to keep

track of your food consumption. Install this on your smartphone or laptop.

19 - Conclusion

Your responsibilities include making the right decisions when it comes to the food you eat, staying healthy and managing health complications while you recover. Keep your kitchen organized so you can eat healthily. Learn the different ways to cook and prepare healthy and nutritious foods. Manage health complications after the surgery. Achieve your goals and be healthy for the rest of your life.

Again, this is a long-term commitment. Along the way, you might commit mistakes in choosing the food to eat, the liquid to drink or the alternatives to the food ingredients you cook. Make your mistakes as learning opportunities to become more cautious. Your journals will aid you in improving your healthy lifestyle.

The final word is experimenting and exploring different healthy recipes is the key to variety and healthy eating. Actually, you can eat anything as long as it is in smaller portion sizes and at a reduced amount of fats. As long as you eat slowly and drink plenty of liquids, you are doing fine. Lastly, always have a follow-up check-up with your doctors. They know what to do when you are uncertain of everything.

Thank You

As we reach the end of this book, I want to say thanks for reading this book.

I want to get this information out to as many people as possible. If you found this book helpful, I would greatly appreciate you leaving me a review. This helps others find the book as well.

Disclaimer

This document is geared towards providing exact and reliable information in regards to the topic and issue covered. The publication is sold on the idea that the publisher is not required to render an accounting, officially permitted, or otherwise, qualified services. If advice is necessary, legal, financial, medical or professional, a practiced individual in the profession should be ordered.

This information is not presented by a financial or medical practitioner and is for entertainment, educational and informational purposes only. The content is not intended as a substitute for professional medical advice, diagnosis, or treatment. Always seek the advice of your physician or other qualified health care provider with any questions you may have regarding a medical condition. Never disregard professional medical advice or delay in seeking it because of something you have read.

The information provided herein is stated to be truthful and consistent, in that any liability, in terms of inattention or otherwise, by any usage or abuse of any policies, processes, or directions contained within is the solitary and utter responsibility of the recipient reader. Under no circumstances

DISCLAIMER

will any legal responsibility or blame be held against the publisher for any reparation, damages, or monetary loss due to the information herein, either directly or indirectly.

Last Updated: 23.Dec.2017